"*A Mom's Ultimate Book of Lists* is *the* book moms have been waiting for! With her solid research and reliable information, Michelle LaRowe has gone from Nanny of the Year to Mom of the Year. *A Mom's Ultimate Book of Lists* should be at the top of every mom's reading list!"

Lynne M. Kenney, PsyD, The Family Coach, North Scottsdale Pediatrics, www.lynnekenney.com

"Michelle LaRowe's book is perfect! It's concise, easy to read, and anxiety-reducing!"

Joan Goldner, president, About Your Time LLC, publisher of BusyBodyBook Organizers

"Let's face it, motherhood is not quite as simple and easy as we imagined it would be when we were kids. *A Mom's Ultimate Book of Lists* is a one-stop resource for finding answers to every parent's questions. From preparing for your baby's arrival, to health, safety, and saving money, Michelle LaRowe covers it all! Through her experience as both a professional nanny and a mother, Michelle offers sound wisdom for the variety of needs in a mom's life. Every mom will want to have this book on her shelf for handy reference and important information that will help her be a positive and wise influence in her home."

Karol Ladd, author of *The Power of a Positive Mom*

A MOM'S
ULTIMATE
BOOK OF LISTS

A MOM'S ULTIMATE
BOOK OF LISTS

100+ LISTS TO SAVE YOU TIME, MONEY, AND SANITY

Michelle LaRowe

Revell

a division of Baker Publishing Group
Grand Rapids, Michigan

Published by Revell
a division of Baker Publishing Group
P.O. Box 6287, Grand Rapids, MI 49516-6287
www.revellbooks.com

Printed in the United States of America

Library of Congress Cataloging-in-Publication Data
LaRowe, Michelle R.
    A mom's ultimate book of lists : 100+ lists to save you time, money, and sanity / Michelle LaRowe.
        p.   cm.
    Includes bibliographical references.
    ISBN 978-0-8007-3382-7 (pbk.)
    1. Motherhood. 2. Parenthood. 3. Child rearing. I. Title.
HQ759.L3722 2009
649'.10242—dc22   2009033565

10   11   12   13   14   15   16   7   6   5   4   3   2   1

To Abby and Jeff,
who are always at the top of my list!

Contents

Lists for the First Year

Lists for the Toddler Years

Lists for the Preschool Years

Lists for Family and Friends

Lists for General Health and Safety

Lists for Saving Your Time, Money, and Sanity

Acknowledgments

It only seems fitting in this book of lists to include the list of those who have made this book possible.

1. God, who has done more for me than I ever deserved or dreamed.
2. My husband Jeff, the best husband and co-parent in the world, who works all day then happily cares for our daughter at night so I have time to read, write, and rewrite.
3. My daughter Abigail, who always gives me inspiration and something to smile about. I love being her mom.
4. My mom Linda, who faithfully cares for Abigail one day a week, allowing me to successfully work from home.
5. My agent Greg Johnson, who is amazingly gifted and talented at what he does. His support, guidance, and encouragement allow me to keep doing what I love to do.
6. Becky Johnson, for teaching me how to "show rather than tell," for believing in my list book concept, and for really teaching me how to write for publication.

7. Jennifer Leep, who took a chance on me and my project and saw it through to the end.
8. Lindsey Spoolstra, who oversaw the editing of this project and made it come to life.
9. The team at Revell, who gave 100 percent to designing, editing, marketing, and selling this book. Your attention to detail has made this book great.
10. The families I've worked with over the years, who have let me into their lives. I've learned a lot by being in the trenches with you and sharing in your daily joys and struggles.
11. The International Nanny Association (INA), who tirelessly works to support nannies and to raise the professional bar for in-home child care. The recognition INA gave me opened the doors for me to write books. It's also because of INA that I am able to be a work-from-home mom.
12. My friends and family, who listen to my never-ending flow of ideas and theories and who always give me honest feedback and encouragement.

Introduction

It wasn't so long ago that I made the exciting and eye-opening transition from nannyhood to motherhood. For more than a decade, I've dedicated my time, energy, and heart to partnering with parents in raising their children. A part of me still can't believe that it was possible for my heart to be filled with more love than I'd already given to and received from the precious children who have called me Nanny.

Pregnant and nervous, I looked back over the years and wondered if my experiences would really prepare me for the 24/7 role of a lifetime called motherhood.

While there was more love than I ever anticipated flowing between me and my newborn daughter, nothing could have prepared me for the tidal wave of emotion that came with having a child of my very own. As much as I've loved the babies I've cared for in years past, there's something special about looking into pools of dark brown eyes and seeing a "mini-me." Perhaps it was the recognition of the child I once was, staring back at me with such innocence, that made having my own baby an experience unlike caring for another woman's child. Or it could be the fact that she was ours, always, to keep and cherish forever, that made being a mom so beautifully unique. Whatever the reason may be, two simple facts remain. We are now the parents in charge of a new life, and it is both fabulous and, at times, frightening.

And while many things have changed now that I have a child of my very own, there are a few things that haven't. True to my "just give me the facts" personality, I am still hungry for the most up-to-date, reliable parenting information. I want to know what's safe and what's not, what is best for my child, and, yes, what exactly is the "normal" time for her to walk, talk, and potty.

Then there is my love of record keeping and resource gathering. In each new nanny position, I've found it necessary to update my research and gather into one special place the most pertinent parenting information that all families need. For me, that special place has always been the family binder.

The family binder has served as an information resource hub, providing the answers to the most commonly asked parenting questions (such as, How many ounces of formula should my newborn be drinking? or, When should a toddler stop napping?); basic medical information (proper dosages of Tylenol, names and descriptions of common childhood illnesses); general health and safety guidelines for children (appropriate car seat choices, toy recommendations for toddlers, and a list of hidden household hazards that need safeguarding); and ideas for age-appropriate activities and outings.

As I spent countless hours gathering and reviewing expert information from such reliable sources as the American Academy of Pediatrics and The Center for Disease Control (among others) while preparing for the birth of my daughter, I couldn't help but think, *Wow. This book would be a lifesaver and time-saver for any new parent.* And that's where the seed of this book in your hand began to sprout.

If you're holding this book, you can say good-bye to the scattered handouts, computer printouts, hand scribbled notes, piles of parenting magazines, overflowing library (that's mostly collecting dust), and any other literature that you've earmarked specifically for gleaning that one piece of (often outdated) information, and say hello to my version of the universal family binder, a one-stop practical resource guide that will you save you time, money, and sanity.

I have to admit that this book is my secret favorite (although my first book, *Nanny to the Rescue*, comes in a close second)! By nature, I am a self-admitted lover of lists and organization. I live by lists and I brake for the Container Store. At any given time, I am armed with grocery lists, shopping lists, or task lists. In fact, people pay me to help them prioritize their lives with lists. So nothing could be more fun and give me more pleasure than writing *A Mom's Ultimate Book of Lists*, which contains 112 of the most practical lists for all moms to live by. This book includes (in an easy-to-find layout) the most sought after parenting information and organizes it into the ultimate practical reference guide for mothers parenting children from birth to age 5. And it even has a whole section dedicated to preparing the mother-to-be for her own up and coming starring role in motherhood.

A Mom's Ultimate Book of Lists really does give you all the information you'll need, minus the hours spent surfing the Internet or searching through bookstores. And it's not just *any* information that you'll find in this resource guide. Because I've done the research for you, *A Mom's Ultimate Book of Lists* provides the most current guidelines; award-winning books, toys, entertainment; and the most practical parenting information in an easy-to-read list format.

Enjoy flipping through this handy, comprehensive guide. You now have all the information you ever wanted to know, literally, at your fingertips.

LISTS FOR PREPARING FOR BABY

1 Common Pregnancy Symptoms and Solutions

In addition to the telltale signs of a missed period and a pregnancy test to confirm that you're expecting, there are some other, often subtle signs that can clue you in to the big news. While these early signs of pregnancy can sometimes be easy to miss, there are other symptoms that will boldly come and go throughout your pregnancy, and still others that may linger persistently until you give birth.

- *Implantation bleeding.* Some women experience light spotting and minimal cramping 6–12 days after conception, as the embryo burrows itself into the uterine wall.
- *Changes in breasts.* A noticeable change in breasts can often be detected as early as 1–2 weeks after conception. For many women, swollen and sore breasts are what lead them to take a home pregnancy test. As pregnancy progresses, the tissue around the nipple—the areola—may become darker. Wearing a supportive bra during the day and a soft cotton sports bra at night (and while sleeping) can help to alleviate discomfort.
- *Extreme fatigue.* As early as one week after conception, many mothers-to-be notice a significant decrease in energy. Be sure to rest as much as you can and stay well hydrated and nourished.
- *Morning sickness.* As early as two weeks after conception, many women experience their first bouts of

queasiness. Morning sickness can occur at any time throughout the day. To stave off vomiting and nausea, snack on crackers before getting out of bed and eat small, frequent meals throughout the day. Talk to your doctor about taking Tums to help relieve a sour stomach or try sucking on some lemon drops for an all-natural cure.

- *Backaches.* A lingering, dull backache (often starting just weeks after conception) can accompany pregnancy. Avoid staying in one position for too long, as doing so can increase tension and pain. Placing a rolled pillow behind your back when sitting and placing a pillow between your legs when sleeping on your side can help relieve pain and pressure. Consider wearing a maternity support belt (found at any maternity store) later in pregnancy to support your growing belly and to help take the pressure off of your back.

- *Heartburn.* During pregnancy hormones can cause the valve between the stomach and the espophagus to relax. When this happens, acid can readily escape from the stomach into the esophagus, causing discomfort and pain. As your uterus grows, it presses on the stomach, making matters worse. Eating small, frequent meals and avoiding acidic or fatty foods and carbonated and caffeinated beverages can help prevent heartburn. Sitting up after you eat can also help to keep food down in the stomach, where it belongs.

- *Swollen feet.* An increase in fluid and a decrease in circulation, compounded by the effects of gravity, can cause feet to swell during pregnancy. Put your feet up as much as possible during the day. If swelling is significant, talk to your doctor about wearing supportive stockings.

- *Constipation.* An increase in hormones and an increase in iron from prenatal vitamins can make your stool less frequent or hard. Upping your fiber intake, exercising regularly, and drinking lots of water can help combat constipation. You may also want to speak with your physician about taking a stool softener, which can offer significant relief.

- *Leg cramps.* Changes in circulation and the weight of your growing belly put pressure on the nerves and blood vessels that run through your legs and can cause leg cramps. Flexing your foot by pulling your toes toward your knee can help stop a painful calf cramp.

- *Groin pain.* Some women experience a sharp, shooting pain in their groin during pregnancy, resulting from the stretching of the round ligaments in that area. Take slow, deep breaths and sit or lie down until the ache passes.

- *Headaches.* Since hormones run at an all-time high during pregnancy, many women experience headaches as their body adjusts to hormonal changes. Be sure to stay well hydrated and talk to your doctor about taking acetaminophen (Tylenol) to relieve the pain.

- *Frequent trips to the bathroom.* From one month post-conception and on, your bladder may be in overdrive, forcing you to visit the bathroom much more often than usual. Scout out places along your commute at which you're comfortable making a pitstop, and always ask an employee where the bathrooms are located when visiting a new venue.

- *Food cravings.* It's no myth; food cravings can often be an early indicator of pregnancy. Don't overdo it on junk food, but allow yourself to satisfy your urge with small portions of what you're craving.

Preggie Pop Drops

Preggie Pop Drops are all-natural, candy-like drops that help curb morning sickness. Flavored with essential oils, they are available in sour fruit flavors, ginger, lavender, and mint. In addition to helping calm a troubled tummy, they also effectively alleviate dry mouth, a common symptom of pregnancy.

▌▌▐▌▌ What's Safe and What's
2 Not during Pregnancy

Every woman wonders about safety during pregnancy. While a lot of the decision making about what is safe for you and your baby comes down to a personal choice, decided by weighing out the benefits and the potential risks of an action, there are some guidelines that women having a healthy, uncomplicated pregnancy can follow to assure that they and their babies stay safe. Always talk with your obstetrical care provider about your safety concerns during pregnancy.

Is It Safe?

Safe	Unsafe, Questionable, or Best to Avoid
Medication	
acetaminophen (Tylenol)[1]	ibuprofen (Motrin)
Tums	
prenatal vitamins	
Talk to your doctor before taking any over the counter or prescription medications.	Talk to your doctor before taking any over the counter or prescription medications.
Nutrition	
sucralose (*Splenda*)[2]	saccharin (*Sweet and Low*)[3]
	Stevia[4]
aspartame (*Equal, NutraSweet*)[5]	raw meat
	deli meat
	sushi
	tuna

24

Safe	Unsafe, Questionable, or Best to Avoid
	shark
	all mercury-containing fish
	smoked fish
	raw shellfish
	raw eggs
	unpasteurized soft cheeses
	unpasteurized milk
	paté
	caffeine
	alcohol
	unwashed vegetables
	unwashed fruits
	herbs
	unpasteurized juices
Exercise	
walking	contact sports
swimming	inherently dangerous sports
aerobics	exercise that requires you to be flat on your back after second trimester
	horseback riding
	heavy weight lifting
Beauty	
perfumes, in moderation	hair coloring
occasional manicures at a hygienic salon	acne treatments
occasional pedicures at a hygienic salon	salicylic acid
acrylic nails applied in a well-ventilated and sanitary salon	mud bath
standard facial	teeth whitening
	skin peels
	saunas
Recreation	
air travel	amusement rides
train travel	hot tubs
cruises	roller coasters
	international travel

	Safe	Unsafe, Questionable, or Best to Avoid
Home		
	baking soda, vinegar, and other natural cleaners	painting
		using pesticides
		lifting heavy things
		fumigating sprays
	chemically based cleaners used according to instructions in a well ventilated area while wearing protective gloves	using chemically based cleaning products in a poorly ventilated area
		litter boxes
		oven cleaner
Lifestyle		
	teeth cleaning	abuse of prescription medications
		illicit drug use
		exposure to radiation
		smoking

Use Your Noggin

Weighing the benefits and risks of an action can help you determine if a decision is right for you. While it may not be ideal to get an X-ray during pregnancy, you and your doctor may decide that determining if you have pneumonia outweighs the risks associated with a limited and controlled onetime exposure to radiation.

While it may be "safe" to get a set of acrylic nails put on while you're pregnant, it's not so safe to get them done by an untrained employee in a poorly ventilated, unsanitary salon.

If you're not sure if something is safe, ask your obstetrical care provider. You and your physician can discuss the potential risks and work through a decision together.

If you're ordered to bed rest, follow the doctor's orders. Ask family, friends, and church members to help you through this tough time. From caring for your other kids to making meals for your family, they'll really be glad they can help. If your family doesn't live nearby, they could send gift cards for restaurants with take-out service—so your husband could pick up dinner on his way home. Also, places like Super Supper will allow you to pick up preassembled frozen dinners that need only to be popped in the oven. The price is reasonable and the ingredients are generally nutritious—and much more tasty than store-bought frozen dinners.

Be Guided by Comfort

Just because something is safe, doesn't mean that you should do it. If you're not comfortable sitting three hours in a cramped and stuffy airplane, don't fly. Being comfortable can help keep stress levels low and limit the aches and pains that can make pregnancy unbearable.

3 Your Changing Body and Developing Baby

The pregnancy journey is filled with emotional and physical changes, but what's really happening with your body and your baby during these nine months?

The First Trimester

Month 1: Weeks 1–4

Your pregnancy is actually dated from the first day of your last menstrual cycle.

About fourteen days before your next period is due, you ovulated.

Anytime within twenty-four hours of ovulation, you could have conceived.

The egg and sperm met, traveled down the fallopian tube, and implanted in the uterus.

The implanted "baby" is called a blastocyst and measures just a few millimeters in length.

A yolk sac forms and will support the pregnancy until the placenta forms.

Your body has detected that it's pregnant and chemical changes have begun to occur.

You stopped ovulating.

You may have begun to wonder if you're pregnant.

You have probably taken an at-home pregnancy test to confirm your pregnancy.

During the first trimester, you can expect to gain between 1 and 1.5 pounds per month.

You may experience early pregnancy symptoms like sore breasts, headaches, or backaches.

Month 2: Weeks 5–8

The blastocyst has now developed into an embryo.

Your baby's heart has begun to beat.

By the end of this month, limb buds will be formed.

By the end of this month, organ development will have begun.

Your baby now measures between 0.31 to 0.43 inches from crown to rump.

By the end of this month, you can see the heart beating during an ultrasound scan.

This month you may begin to feel pregnant, and morning sickness and fatigue may have set in.

You may feel nervous, excited, or anxious.

Month 3: Weeks 9–12

This month marks the beginning of the fetal period.

During this month your baby's bones will begin to harden.

An ultrasound this month may show lots of movement.

The external genitalia are now beginning to differentiate.

It is still difficult to determine your baby's gender through ultrasound.

Your baby's head is about half the size of his or her body.

Your baby may weigh about 0.49 ounces.

Your baby may measure in at nearly 3.5 inches.

You may begin to experience heartburn.

You may notice that you have sudden mood swings.

The Second Trimester

Month 4: Weeks 13–16

You can expect to gain .5 to .75 pounds per week this trimester.

The placenta has now taken over and is providing nourishment to your baby.

Your baby is now urinating and is making some of its own insulin and bile.

Your baby is pumping nearly 25 quarts of blood per day.

Your baby's teeth have even formed.

Your baby weighs in at about 3 ounces and measures in at about 6.3 inches.

You may now be able to determine the gender of your baby via ultrasound.

You're probably really beginning to feel pregnant.

You may begin to need maternity clothing.

You may begin to have the "pregnancy glow," as the amount of blood you're circulating increases.

Month 5: Weeks 17–20

If this is not your first pregnancy, you may now be able to notice your baby's movements.

New organs are forming and your baby is developing fingerprints.

Fine hair called lanugo now covers your baby.

Your baby weighs about 10 ounces.

Your baby is approximately 9.8 inches in total length.

You may feel dizzy if you change positions too quickly.

You may have sharp pains in your groin area as the round ligaments are stretching.

Month 6: Weeks 21–24

Your baby is now doing practice breathing.

You may begin to notice your baby's movements.

Fat is being deposited under your baby's skin, which will help with temperature regulation at birth.

Your baby now weighs 1.5 pounds.

Your baby is now about 11.8 inches in total length.

Babies born at 24 weeks can sometimes survive with intensive medical care.

You may begin to feel better and have more energy.

You may have leg cramps.

You may begin to have trouble sleeping.

Month 7: Weeks 25–28

Your baby's movements are probably now unmistakable.

You may notice that your baby has distinguishable sleep and wake patterns.

You're beginning to feel really uncomfortable.

You may experience constipation.

It may be hard to get into a comfortable sleep position.

Your baby weighs about 2.4 pounds.

Your baby is about 13.8 inches long.

Babies born this early can often survive if they have advanced medical support.

The Third Trimester

Month 8: Weeks 29–32

You can expect to gain about 1 pound per week this trimester.

You may be asked to do fetal kick counts to monitor your baby's activity.

Your baby is getting ready for birth and is growing rapidly.

Your baby is circulating nearly 300 quarts of blood a day.

On average, babies now weigh about 3 pounds and 11 ounces.

On average, babies now measure 15.8 inches.

By the end of this month, your baby is doing everything he or she will do after birth, except cry.

Your baby is in a state of maturing.

You may begin to nest, having the desire to clean and organize everything.

Month 9: Weeks 33–36

Your baby's lungs are maturing.

Your baby's lungs are secreting surfactant, which will help them expand when the baby is born.

The average birth weight of babies is 7.5 pounds.

The average length of babies at birth is 18–22 inches.

You may get practice contractions, also called Braxton Hicks contractions.

By the end of this month, your uterus is about 6.5 inches from your navel.

Months 10 and 11: Weeks 37–42

Your baby is gaining coordination and getting ready for his or her birth day.

You may notice that your baby drops lower into your pelvis.

Weight gain may cease and you may even lose a pound or two.

You'll probably experience false labor.

You are probably ready to be done being pregnant.

By the Numbers

A normal pregnancy lasts between 37 and 42 weeks.

Only 4 percent of babies are actually born on their due date.

6–10 percent of babies are born early—prior to 37 weeks.

4–14 percent of pregnancies last more than 42 weeks.[6]

Calculating Your Due Date

The standard due date calculation is called Nägele's Rule. This rule was developed in the 1850s by Dr.

Nägele, who determined that the average human pregnancy lasts 266 days from conception, or 280 days (40 weeks) from the first day of the last menstrual period. This calculation does not account for women who don't know the precise date of their last period or women who have longer or shorter menstrual cycles.

To calculate your due date, take the first day of your last period (LMP) and add 7 days. Then subtract 3 months. LMP + 7 days − 3 months = Expected Date of Delivery. Example: January 1 + 7 days − 3 months = October 8.

How many months in a pregnancy and how are trimesters divided?

A pregnacy is considered full term at 40 weeks.

Some women calculate their due date by the lunar calendar, which defines a month as 4 weeks. They take 40 weeks and divide it by 4 weeks per month to calculate a 10-month pregnancy.

Other women calculate their due date using the Gregorian calendar. Starting with the date they began their period, they count one month of pregnancy from that date to the same date of the next month. If you started your period on January 15, on March 15 you'd be 2 months pregnant. Using this method, pregnancy lasts 9 months.

The most common and most accurate way to calculate your due date is using Nägele's Rule.

This difference in calculations is also the reason why some resources use different weeks to define when a trimester starts and ends. A trimester is technically defined as a term of three months.[7]

▌▌▐▌▌ Routine Tests Offered
4 during Pregnancy

In addition to being weighed and having your belly measured regularly throughout your pregnancy, you will have lots of screenings and testing. During your pregnancy, it's important that you understand what tests and screenings are being offered and why they are recommended. Talk to your obstetrical care provider prior to any testing to be sure you give informed consent.

Routine Tests and Screenings

Test	When It's Typically Done	What It Tests For	How It's Done
Rh factor	first appointment	blood type	blood draw
Hematocrit	first appointment	low red blood count (anemia)	blood draw
CBC	first appointment	blood health	blood draw
Hepatitis B	first appointment	hepatitis B	blood draw
RPR	first appointment	syphilis	blood draw
HIV	first appointment	HIV	blood draw
Immunity to rubella	first appointment	immunity to German measles	blood draw
Immunity to varicella	first appointment	immunity to chicken pox	blood draw
Cervical test	first appointment	STDs and cervical abnormalities	Pap smear
Blood pressure	every appointment	high or low blood pressure	pressure cuff
Urinalysis	every appointment	sugar, protein, and infection	urine dip
Sickle-cell anemia	anytime during pregnancy	blood disease in women of African and Mediterranean descent	blood draw
Baby's heart rate	after heartbeat is confirmed	heart rate of baby	using a Doppler or fetal scope

Test	When It's Typically Done	What It Tests For	How It's Done
Ultrasound	18–20 weeks, as ordered	fetal growth and development	ultrasound scan
Glucose screening	24–28 weeks, as ordered	gestational diabetes	blood draw or series of blood draws following a sugary drink
Group B strep	between 35 and 37 weeks	streptococcus infection	vaginal/rectal swab
Biophysical profile	as ordered	health of baby	ultrasound scan
Nonstress test	as ordered	heart rate of baby	wearing a belt with heart rate and uterine contraction monitors attached
Contraction stress test	as ordered	effects of contractions on fetal heart rate	wearing a belt with heart rate and uterine contraction monitors attached; Pitocin may be given
Umbilical artery Doppler	as ordered	blood flow to placenta	ultrasound scan

Genetic Testing and Screening

> But those who suffer he delivers in their suffering; he speaks to them in their affliction.
>
> Job 36:15

Often women over age thirty-five and women with a family history of genetic or chromosomal abnormalities are encouraged to pursue genetic testing. This testing can be used to diagnose disease, direct treatments, and prepare parents for the challenge of parenting a child with special needs. For people of faith, who tend to embrace a culture of life, genetic testing can be a valuable tool to enrich and improve life, but most Christians would not consider terminating a life because testing revealed that something was awry.

It's also important to note that while some genetic tests (amniocentesis, for example) can accurately reveal if there is a serious problem with your developing baby, other prentatal genetic "tests" (like the triple or quad screen) are simply screening tests and cannot be used to diagnose a problem, but instead are used to calculate your baby's risk of having a particular problem. Some babies who are calculated to have a high risk for a particular problem are born with no problems at all.

Genetic Testing and Screenings Routinely Offered

Test/Screening	When It's Done	What It Does	How It's Done
Cystic fibrosis	first appointment	diagnostic test for the cystic fibrosis gene	blood draw
Chronic villus sampling	weeks 10–12	diagnostic test for genetic disorders, chromosomal abnormalities, or defects	cervical suction or abdominal needle
Nuchal translucency	weeks 11–14	screening test for birth defects, abnormalities, and congenital heart problems	ultrasound scan
Amniocentesis	usually done between weeks 14–20 but may be done as early as week 11 or as ordered thereafter	diagnostic test for chromosome abnormalities, genetic disorders and defects, and lung maturity	abdominal needle
First Trimester Screen	weeks 11–13	screening test for risk of chromosome abnormalities	blood draw, ultrasound scan
Triple Screen	weeks 15–20	screening test for risk of birth defects and chromosome abnormalities	blood draw
Quad Screen	weeks 16–18	screening test for risk of birth defects and chromosome abnormalities	blood draw

For you created my inmost being; you knit me together in my mother's womb. I praise you because I am fearfully and wonderfully made; your works are wonderful, I know that full well. My frame was not hidden from you when I was made in the secret place. When I was woven together in the depths of the earth, your eyes saw my unformed body. All the days ordained for me were written in your book before one of them came to be.

Psalm 139:13–16

5 When to Call the Doctor

While aches and pains during pregnancy are to be expected, there are some symptoms that you just shouldn't ignore. If you are experiencing any of these symptoms, call your obstetrical care provider immediately.

Symptom	Reason Not to Ignore
Extreme vomiting	Could cause severe dehydration
Vaginal bleeding	Could indicate a variety of things, from nothing to a tear in the placenta
Abdominal pain	Could signal ectopic pregnancy or other issues
Cramping	Could indicate nothing or a variety of issues
Watery discharge	Could indicate a ruptured amniotic sac
Contractions	Could be a sign of preterm labor
Severe headaches	Could indicate high blood pressure or other issues including preeclampsia
Excessive swelling	Could indicate high blood pressure or other issues including preeclampsia
Decrease of fetal movement	Could indicate that the baby is in distress
Fever	Could indicate a viral illness or bacterial infection
Severe leg pain	Could indicate blood clots in deep leg veins

Don't Be Afraid to Call the Doctor

Never worry that you'll be a bother by calling the doctor with your questions or concerns. In most cases, a quick exam or a simple medical test can ease your anxiety and worries. A good obstetrician or midwife will tell you that he or she never wants a patient to sit home and worry.

6 Ten Things to Think About When Considering Adoption

1. *Your motive for adopting.* Think about why you want to adopt. Is it because you have a deep desire to be a parent and want to let the love of God pour through you into a child's heart? Are you hoping a child will mend a broken marriage? It's important to evaluate the reasons you're pursuing adoption so you can identify and work through any unhealthy motives.
2. *Your spouse's interest in adoption.* Be sure to have lengthy discussions with your spouse about adopting. Talk about how it will impact your lives, lifestyle, finances, and working situations. Be honest about your feelings and pray together about how to proceed.
3. *Your family and friends may not understand or embrace your decision.* Adoption is a personal decision that is not right for everyone. Some people may not understand your choice or offer their unconditional support. Pray for grace to handle these situations and come to an agreement on how you will share the news with family and friends.

4. *Your finances.* Chances are you'll need to plan and budget for your adoption expenses. Now is a great time to implement a family budget. Look for ways to cut back, save, and raise financial support. Be sure to research grants available for adoptive parents.

5. *Having an honest adoption process.* Adoption case workers will want to know everything about you, including the things you'd prefer to keep to yourself. Pray for transparency and the confidence to be your true self. Be prepared to share your story of how you've overcome personal struggles and tragedy.

6. *The type of child that you wish to adopt.* Pray about what child God would have you parent. Consider if you have the skills to parent a child with special needs or the finances and space to take in a sibling pair. Do you want to adopt domestically or internationally? Ask God to show you the child he has for you. Find out ahead of time any particulars about the child's environment that may have inhibited normal bonding abilities. Did the baby have fetal alcohol syndrome? These issues may lead to some long-term complications and specialized care needs. Don't close your eyes to potential problems but find out all you can and gather resources to help should you adopt a baby with special needs.

7. *Issues that have prevented you from becoming pregnant.* Have you struggled with infertility and consciously made the decision to be a parent, rather than be pregnant? If you're single and are adopting alone, are you disappointed that you'll be parenting solo? Talk to God about your joys, disappointments, and frustrations and trust him to give you a fresh, new perspective.

8. *Adopting an older child.* Although you may plan on adopting a baby, consider the joy and excitement that an older child can bring. Ask God if he's called you to help heal a hurting heart and provide unconditional

love, support, and acceptance to a child who may have known only pain, disappointment, and rejection.

9. *The differences between you and your adopted child.* You may not have the same skin, eye, or hair color, but you have the same heart. Ask God to help you embrace the differences that you and your child may have and consider ways that you could help an adopted child stay connected to his or her heritage.

10. *Things may not go as planned.* Delays, new adoption laws, and even last minute changes of heart can occur. Prepare yourself to withstand the adoption process and the heartache that the change of plans may cause. Know that "God causes everything to work together for the good of those who love God and are called according to his purpose for them" (Rom. 8:28 NLT).

Christian Adoption Resources

The Adoption Decision: 15 Things You Want to Know Before Adopting by Laura Christianson

Successful Adoption: A Guide for Christian Families by Natalie Nichols Gillespie

Adoption in the Bible

Joseph adopted Jesus.
Pharaoh's daughter adopted Moses.
Mordecai adopted Esther.
God adopted *you*!

Not only so, but we ourselves, who have the firstfruits of the Spirit, groan inwardly as we wait eagerly for our adoption as sons, the redemption of our bodies.

Romans 8:23

▮▮▮▮ Ten Things to Think About
7 When Expecting Multiples

According to the American College of Obstetrics and Gynecologists, one out of every forty-one births is a birth of twins. While parents who are expecting single babies can often get away with "winging it" through their pregnancy and plans for new baby care, mothers of multiples can benefit from giving some pregnancy and parenting issues a little extra forethought. And while "the more the merrier" can certainly be true in homes of higher order multiples, for moms of triplets, quads, and more, additional planning and preparation is essential for early parenting success.

1. *The probability of bed rest.* The chances that you'll be ordered to bed go up when carrying more than one baby, because of the increased side effects and risks of complications.
2. *The possibility of preterm labor.* Multiple pregnancies have an increased risk of preterm labor and other complications.
3. *An increased risk of cesarean section.* Learn about cesarean delivery and have help on standby to assist you in caring for your family during recovery.
4. *Breastfeeding multiples.* You'll need to eat about five hundred additional calories per day if you plan to breastfeed your twins—and more for triplets or quads. You may want to meet with a lactation consultant prior to giving birth to discuss techniques for nursing two or more.
5. *Things you'll need two of.* Sometimes you'll need two, and sometimes one will do. Save your money and sanity

41

by getting only the equipment you know you'll need (see List 30).

6. *Scheduling.* Managing multiples works best when your babies are on a sleeping and feeding schedule. Plan to keep a record of who does what and when, to avoid mix-ups.

7. *Routines.* Establishing a workable routine can help assure that everyone gets what he or she needs every day. From getting everyone bathed to getting everyone out of the house, having a system in place can make things easier.

8. *Getting help.* When caring for your newborns, it can be great to have others pitch in by preparing meals, cleaning house, and helping to care for older children. Don't be shy. Ask for help by specifying how you could really use it.

9. *Sleeping arrangements.* To maximize your rest, consider sharing a room with your newborns. In a tight space, a co-sleeper that attaches to the bed is a wonderful alternative to a crib.

10. *How you'll dress them.* If you're having two of the same gender, you may want to give some thought as to whether to dress your multiples alike. Coordinating your multiples' clothing can be a great alternative to dressing them identically.

Ways to Save

Many companies offer "freebies" to mothers of multiples. Call the customer service numbers of your favorite companies and ask if they provide samples of their products to mothers of multiples.

Many stores, like Stride Rite and OshKosh B'Gosh, offer discounts to parents of multiples. Savings usually come in a percentage off a second item purchased.

Also check out local Mothers of Twins clubs for additional money saving resources (www.nomotc.org).

Signs of Preterm Labor

Call your obstetrical care provider immediately if you notice:

✓ contractions that occur more than four to six times per hour
✓ a low, dull backache
✓ pelvic pressure
✓ diarrhea
✓ vaginal bleeding or spotting
✓ watery discharge

8 Key Components to Include in Your Maternity Leave Proposal

If you're going to return to work after the birth of your baby, planning your maternity leave can be a stressful task. From determining how much time you can afford to take off, to researching the ins and outs of your company's maternity related benefits, to presenting your maternity leave proposal to your employer, you'll need a well-thought-out strategic plan to make things sail smoothly.

A well-written maternity leave proposal can help maximize the chances that you'll get what you need to make your maternity leave successful and can minimize the effects that your leave will have on your co-workers and employer.

A well-thought-out maternity leave proposal should include:

✓ the date you intend to start your leave

✓ the duration of your leave

✓ the types of leave you plan to take and the order you'll be taking them (vacation, unpaid leave, and so on)

✓ the date you anticipate returning to work

✓ a list of responsibilities that will be affected because of your leave

✓ a list of people who will be affected by your leave

✓ suggestions for how affected responsibilities and people should be handled

✓ how you'd like to communicate with your place of employment while you're away

What You Need to Know

Workplace policies. Become familiar with the policies and procedures your employer has for requesting and taking maternity leave.

The Pregnancy Discrimination Act. Employers with at least 15 workers cannot fire (or refuse to hire) you because of your pregnancy. This law also mandates that pregnant women be allowed to work as long as they can perform their duties. The act requires that once you're on maternity leave, your job must be held open for you.

Family and Medical Leave Act (FMLA). FMLA requires companies that employ more than 50 people in a 75-mile radius (or any and all government workers) to provide up to 12 weeks of unpaid leave during any 12-month period to eligible employees (employees that have worked 1,250 hours in a 12-month period) for the birth and care of a newborn, for placement of a foster or adoptive child, or to care for oneself or an immediate family member with a serious health condition.[8] Men are also eligible for unpaid leave under FMLA, but if you and your spouse work for the same company, you are limited to a combined total of 12 weeks of leave per year. You may not qualify under FMLA if you are in the top 10 percent of earners in your company or if, by keeping your position open during your absence, the company will suffer significant financial loss.

Your state's maternity leave laws. Some states (including California, New Jersey, and New York) have expanded FMLA laws to provide longer time off and/or paid maternity leave through their state temporary disability insurance programs.[9] In some states the number of FMLA–eligible workers a company must employ for a person to be eligible is reduced, allowing women who work for smaller companies to receive benefits under its law.

Short-Term Disability (STD) Insurance. STD pays a percentage of your salary if you become temporarily disabled and are unable to work due to sickness, pregnancy, or injury. "A typical STD policy provides you with a weekly portion of your salary, usually 50, 60, or 66⅔ percent for 13 to 26 weeks [although 6 weeks seems to be the standard for pregnancy]."[10] If your employer does not offer STD, you can purchase an individual policy directly through an insurance company or agent.

9 What to Include in Your Birthing Plan

Writing a birthing plan gives you the opportunity to outline your labor and delivery requests and to maintain some control during your birthing experience. Drafting a plan also gives you an opportunity to discuss your options and make informed decisions about your labor and delivery with your spouse and your health-care provider during a nonstressful time.

While the Internet, pregnancy books, and advice from your girlfriends and mother can be helpful for gleaning basic information about labor and delivery, your primary sources for information should be your obstetrical care provider.

First-time moms can especially benefit from enrolling in prenatal classes at their local hospital, birthing center, or doctor's office where the staff and curriculum are specifically focused on educating you about the birthing experience.

Although some hospital policies and medical situations may prevent you from having everything go as planned, it's important to think about what matters most to you in the birthing experience. Share your wishes with your health-care team by discussing your desires and by giving each member of your team a copy of your written birthing plan.

Draft your birthing plan using the template below. Include only the items that you've selected.

Basic Information

> your name
> your spouse's name
> your expected due date
> your doctor's name and contact information
> your pediatrician's name and contact information
> the type of birth you are planning (vaginal, cesarean, multiple birth, vaginal birth after a previous cesarean)

Birthing Environment

> ✓ I would like a private room.
> ✓ I would like to have the lights dimmed.
> ✓ I would like it as quiet as possible.

✓ I will be bringing my own music.

✓ I wish to wear my own clothing.

✓ I would like/would not like to have a phone in my room.

✓ I would like/would not like to have visitors during early labor.

✓ I would like to have my partner videotape our labor and birth.

✓ I would like to take pictures during my labor and birth.

✓ I would not like students to be part of my medical team.

✓ I would like to keep the exams by medical personnel to a necessary minimum.

✓ I would like to have continuous access to a shower.

✓ I would like to sit in a birthing tub or pool.

During Labor

✓ I would like to be able to walk around.

✓ I would like to be able to snack.

✓ I would like to be able to drink clear fluids.

✓ I would like to be able to use the bathroom.

✓ I would prefer/prefer not to have a catheter.

✓ I would prefer/prefer not to have an enema.

✓ I would prefer/prefer not to have my pubic hair shaved.

✓ I would like to have ice chips available to me.

✓ I would prefer a heparin/saline lock.

✓ I want an IV only if I become dehydrated.

✓ I would like to choose my birthing positions.

✓ I would prefer to be continuously monitored.

✓ I would prefer to be intermittently monitored.

✓ I would prefer/prefer not to have internal fetal monitoring.

✓ I would prefer to be monitored by an external fetal monitor.

✓ I would prefer to be monitored using a Doppler.

Pain Relief

✓ I am planning a natural childbirth and will be using _____ technique to manage my pain.

✓ I am planning to have an epidural as soon as possible.

✓ I am planning on a natural childbirth, but if I ask for medication I prefer:

    ✓ Stadol

    ✓ Nubain

    ✓ Demerol

    ✓ walking epidural

    ✓ full epidural

Induction

✓ I do not wish to have the amniotic sac artificially ruptured unless it is absolutely necessary.

✓ If labor is not progressing, I would like/would not like to have my amniotic sac artificially ruptured.

✓ I would prefer/prefer not to use Pitocin to induce me.

✓ I would prefer/prefer not to use Cytotec to induce me.

✓ I would prefer/prefer not to use prostaglandin gel to induce me.

Cesarean Section

✓ Unless medically necessary, I do not want a cesarean delivery.

✓ If a cesarean is recommended, and if time permits, I would like a second opinion.

✓ If a cesarean is necessary, I prefer/prefer not to have my spouse or birthing coach present.

Vaginal Delivery

✓ I would like to have a mirror so I can see my baby crowning.

✓ I would like my partner to cut the umbilical cord.

✓ I would like to have my baby on my stomach/chest immediately after birth.

✓ I would like to try to nurse immediately following birth.

✓ I would prefer/prefer not to have people cheering me on as I push.

✓ I would prefer/prefer not to have Pitocin to help me expel the placenta.

✓ I prefer/prefer not to have an episiotomy.

✓ I prefer to tear.

✓ I prefer local anesthesia during an episiotomy repair.

✓ If an assisted birth is necessary I prefer:
  ✓ a vacuum-assisted delivery
  ✓ a forceps-assisted delivery

✓ I plan on banking my cord blood.

Baby Care

- ✓ I would prefer that my baby's vernix be wiped into his or her skin, rather than wiped off.
- ✓ I want/do not want my baby to have a vitamin K shot immediately following birth.
- ✓ I prefer/prefer not to have my baby treated with antibiotic eye ointment immediately following birth.
- ✓ I want/do not want my baby to have standard vaccinations.
- ✓ I plan to breastfeed.
- ✓ I plan to bottle-feed.
- ✓ I plan to use/not use a pacifier.
- ✓ I prefer to room with my baby.
- ✓ I prefer that my baby be cared for in the nursery.
- ✓ I prefer that my spouse or I be with my baby at all times.
- ✓ I do not wish to circumcise my baby.
- ✓ I prefer that my baby be circumcised in the hospital.
- ✓ If my baby must be transported to another facility, we wish to go with him or her as soon as possible.
- ✓ If my baby requires special care, we wish to be active members of his or her care team.

Additional Requests:

_____

_____

_____

_____

_____

_____

Who Should Have a Copy of Your Birth Plan?

your spouse
your obstetrician/midwife
your admitting staff
your labor coach
you, at your bedside

10 Common Pain Medications Used in Childbirth

Each woman and each pregnancy, labor, and delivery is unique, and not every type of pain medication is right for every woman. The use of pain relief during childbirth is a personal decision that should be thoroughly discussed with your health-care provider. Not all methods of pain relief are offered at all birthing facilities, so be sure to talk to your obstetrical care provider early in your pregnancy to become familiar with all of your pain-relieving options.

Types of Medications Used for Pain Relief

Narcotics

Common analgesia narcotics used in childbirth:

meperidine (Demerol)
morphine
fentanyl
butorphanol (Stadol)
nalbuphine (Nubain)[11]

Narcotics are medications that are put into the bloodstream to lessen the intensity of pain and make childbirth more bearable.

Narcotics can be given by IV, by patient controlled analgesia (PCA), or by intramuscular shot.

Narcotics can make you sleepy, nauseous, itchy, or constipated.

Narcotics cross the placenta and enter the baby's bloodstream.

Narcotics can make your baby's heart rate change.

Narcotics can make your baby sleepy after birth.

Regional Anesthesia

Common regional anesthesia used in childbirth:

epidural block

spinal block

combination spinal block and epidural block: "walking epidural"

Regional anesthesia allows the mother to be awake and alert during childbirth.

Regional anesthesia blocks pain signals so that they do not reach the brain.

EPIDURAL BLOCK

A needle is placed into the epidural space outside of the sac containing the spinal fluid and cord, a catheter is inserted through the needle, and the needle is then withdrawn.

An epidural can provide a constant flow of medication.

Epidural medications used can be analgesic or anesthetic.

Epidural medication can be increased or decreased as pain indicates.

An epidural takes full effect in about 10 to 20 minutes.

An epidural may slow the baby's heart rate.

Potential side effects from epidurals, although rare, can include headaches or a decrease in blood pressure.

An epidural may be more effective on one side of the body than the other.

The ideal epidural will still allow you to feel some sensation so that you can actively push during labor.

Spinal Block

A needle is used to inject medication into the sac containing the spinal fluid and cord.[12]

A spinal block is effective for only a few hours.

Only one spinal injection is usually given.

A spinal block combines anesthetics and narcotics.

A spinal block is often used for cesarean deliveries.

Potential side effects from a spinal block, although rare, can include headaches or a decrease in blood pressure.

Local Anesthesia

Local anesthetics are injected into the area between the vagina and the rectum to numb the area.

Local anesthetics are sometimes used to numb the area before an episiotomy.

Local anesthetics are often used to numb the area during episiotomy repair.

Local anesthetics last for short periods of time.

Local anesthetics rarely affect the baby.

Pudendal Block

A pudendal block is given moments before delivery.

A pudendal block is injected into the vaginal wall.

A pudendal block relieves pain temporarily.

A pudendal block is effective in moments.

A pudendal block rarely has negative effects on the mother or baby.

GENERAL ANESTHESIA

General anesthesia is most often used during emergency cesarean sections.

General anesthesia makes you lose consciousness.

General anesthesia can be given via face mask or IV.

Due to a risk of the aspiration of food, general anesthesia is usually given after eight hours of fasting.

Categories of Pain Relief Medication

- An *analgesic* provides full or partial relief of painful sensations without the loss of muscle function.
- An *anesthetic* provides an intense blockage of all sensations including muscle movement.
- A *systematic analgesic* provides pain relief without the loss of consciousness by acting on an entire body system.

Tranquilizers

Tranquilizers are medications used to help decrease anxiety and promote rest in the early stages of labor. They can be given by mouth, by injection, or through IV. Tranquilizers may cause drowsiness, may decrease your memory of labor, and may decrease your baby's activeness after birth. Tranquilizers do not relieve pain.

Natural Tools for Pain Relief

prayer
Lamaze breathing techniques
sitting in a warm bath
massage
changes in position
transcutaneous electrical nerve stimulation (TENS)
relaxation techniques
the Bradley Method of husband-coached childbirth

My help comes from the LORD, the Maker of heaven and earth.

Psalm 121:2

11 Christian Principles for the Successful Single Mother

Raising kids alone is tough. No doubt about it. But fortunately, as Christians, single moms can take heart knowing that they'll never be raising their children truly alone. God is with you, goes before you, and fights on your behalf (Deut. 1:30).

Meditate on the following Christian principles that can help put your parenting role in perspective.

The successful single mother:

- trusts God to be her mate, her provider, her friend, and a father to her children (Isaiah 54:5–6; Psalm 68:5; Philippians 4:19)

- is not too prideful to ask for help (Psalm 138:6; James 4:6)
- loses the single-mom guilt (Romans 8:1; 2 Corinthians 12:8–10)
- trusts God to watch over her children (Psalm 146:9)
- trusts God to help her teach her children (Isaiah 54:13)
- sees herself the way God sees her (Romans 8:1–39)
- knows God loves her children and calls them his own (Isaiah 43:1; John 3:16)
- trains her children in the way of the Lord (Deuteronomy 6:6–7; Proverbs 22:6)
- trusts that God has a plan for her and her children (Jeremiah 29:11)
- lives by faith (2 Corinthians 5:7; Hebrews 11:1)

Resources for Christian Single Moms

On My Own: Help and Hope for Single Moms by Lela Gilbert
Psalm 23 for the Single Parent by Carmen Leal
Single Moms Raising Sons: Preparing Boys to Be Men When There's No Man Around by Dana Chisholm

A Cup of Joy at www.acupofjoy.org
Focus on the Family at www.focusonthefamily.com
Mothers of Preschoolers—MOPS at www.mops.org

I can do everything through him who gives me strength.

Philippians 4:13

12 Preparing for Baby

With so many choices in baby gear available, it can be hard to know what you really need and what you really don't. The following lists can help you navigate the aisles of newborn "necessities" and hone your baby registry so that you can properly prepare for bringing home your bundle.

Diapering

Ideally you want to have a diaper station in each area of the home where you plan to spend lots of time with your baby. A fully stocked basket works well as a secondary diapering station. If you don't have enough store-bought changing pads to go around, you can use a clean towel folded in half for a portable changing location.

What you'll need:

antibacterial hand sanitizer in a pump container
antibacterial hand soap in a pump container
diaper pail and liners or trash bags
diaper rash cream or ointment
high-quality baby wipes
newborn diapers
size 1 diapers
waterproof pads
changing table*

changing table pad*
changing table pad cover*

Bathing, Health, and Hygiene

Your pediatrician (or hospital nurse) will instruct you on how and how often to bathe your baby, but for the first weeks it's usually limited to gentle sponge baths. Be sure to clean your baby's hands, neck, face, and the area behind the ears after each feeding.

What you'll need:

baby emery boards
baby hairbrush
baby wash in pump container
digital thermometer
digital thermometer probe covers
nasal aspirator
newborn nail clippers
ointment for dry skin
petroleum jelly
saline drops
small plastic bucket or bowl
baby bathtub*
baby lotion*
six baby washcloths*
three infant towels*

Feeding

The decision to breastfeed or bottle-feed your baby is a highly personal choice and only you can decide what's best for you and your baby.

UNICEF, the American Academy of Pediatrics, and the World Health Organization recommend that infants be breastfed exclusively for the first 6 months of life.[13]

If you want to nurse your baby but are having difficulty, La Leche League or a local lactation consultant can provide you with the proper support. Your pediatrician or obstetrician can direct you to lactation resources in your area.

Some moms prefer expressing their milk with a pump and bottle-feeding, so they can share the feeding duties with their spouse and other caregivers. Other moms choose to supplement breast milk with infant formula and still others choose to strictly formula feed their babies. There are even moms that do a little of each during the parenting journey. There is no right decision, only a decision that is right for you.

What you'll need:

six or more cloth diapers to use as burp clothes
six or more small cloth bibs

What you'll need for bottle-feeding:

six 4-ounce bottles
six 8-ounce bottles
six fast-flow bottle nipples
six slow-flow bottle nipples
formula (talk to your pediatrican about what type is best
    for your baby)
basket to hold nipples in dishwasher*
bottle drying rack*

bottled water*

nipple brush*

single-serving formula packets or prepared formula for
on-the-go use*

What you'll need for breastfeeding:

nursing bras

nursing pads

hospital quality breast pump and accessories (available
from your local hospital, pharmacy, or medical supply
store)—if pumping

milk storage containers—if pumping

Clothing

It's so tempting to dress your new baby in the loveliest of
outfits, but to make life easier, stick to side-snap cotton T-
shirts, Onesies, one-piece playsuits, sleep gowns, and socks.
Purchasing all white basics will speed up sorting and folding
laundry, and will make stains easier to remove. Be sure to
ask your pediatrician if he or she approves of using diluted
chlorine-free bleach for stain removal on anything that will
touch your baby's skin.

What you'll need:

three newborn gowns

six pairs of infant socks

six sleepers with long sleeves and feet

six T-shirts that snap between the legs (commonly called
by the brand name Onesies)

Bedding

Providing a safe place for your baby to sleep is a parenting priority. In the first months, the safest place for your baby to sleep is in a separate sleep space in the same room as you. At about four months, you may wish to transition your baby to his or her own room. Babies should never be placed in a sleep space with loose blankets or bedding.

What you'll need:

co-sleeping bassinet
two bassinet sheets
crib with firm mattress
a waterproof crib mattress pad
two waterproof crib sheet savers
two crib sheets
six waffle-weave receiving blankets
two swaddle blankets or baby wraps
two sleeping sacks
crib mobile*

Laundry

Always be sure to use laundry detergent, not laundry soap, when washing your baby's clothing. Soap can remove the fire retardant treatment on children's clothing and sleepwear. You may want to consider using a special fragrance/dye free laundry detergent, like Dreft, that is designed specifically for use on baby clothes. If you are concerned for your baby's sensitive skin, you may wish to opt for a laundry detergent that has no dyes, fragrances, or other irritants. These can be purchased at your local Whole Foods store or larger chain grocery store. Having a hamper handy near each diapering station (along with an extra outfit) can be a great time-saver.

What you'll need:

fragrance/dye free laundry detergent
infant hangers
laundry hamper or basket
spray stain remover
small lingerie bag for socks or other small items*

On the Go

If you have the right gear, getting out of the house with your baby will be a breeze. Always keep one fully loaded diaper bag in the car, and keep an extra bottle, formula, wipes, diapers, clothes, blankets, and a towel or two for emergencies or unplanned extended outings in the trunk of your vehicle.

What you'll need:

infant car seat
infant car seat base for each vehicle
stroller frame that accommodates your infant car seat
convertible car seat
two diaper bags, preferably with a built-in changing station[14]
travel case for baby wipes, or individual resealable packages of wipes
high quality umbrella stroller with swivel wheels, five-point harness, and a fully reclining seat
infant car seat cover
basket or handled carrier for item storage in the trunk of your vehicle*
infant front carrier or sling*

portable crib or play yard*
sheet for the portable crib or play yard*
stroller bunting bag or boot*

Gadgets and Furniture

Deciding what you need and what you don't for your nursery can be overwhelming. The following is a list of newborn nursery essentials.

What you'll need:

baby gate—if you have pets or toddlers in the house. (You'll eventually need one or more anyway!)
baby monitor
bouncy seat[15]
clock
crib tent—if you have pets or toddlers in the house
daily logbook to keep track of eating and eliminating patterns
dresser, chest of drawers, or armoire for baby's clothes
flashlight and extra batteries
lamp and dimmer switch (available at home improvement stores)
night-light
trash can
CD player and lullaby CDs*
pacifiers*
changing table*
feeding pillow*
gliding, stuffed chair or comfy padded rocking chair*
ottoman for chair*

swing*
table large enough to hold clock, bottles, and other
    items*
white noise maker*

*Optional

13 Hospital Packing List

Even if you're having a scheduled induction, you just don't
know how long your hospital stay will last, so to be best
prepared, pack for an extended stay. Have your hospital
bags packed and ready to go by the middle of your third
trimester.

Labor Bag

bathrobe*
a copy of your birthing plan*
eyeglasses (if needed)*
insurance card*
lip moisturizer*
list of medications*
slippers*
toiletries, including hairbrush, toothbrush, toothpaste,
    hair elastics, and deodorant*
bottled water**
cell phone**
hard candies**

nightgowns, several that zip or button up**
pillows and colored pillowcases**
reading material**
snacks**
socks, a few pair**
tennis balls or other massage aids**
underwear, several changes**
massage lotion or oil***
music and compact music player (if desired)***
notebook computer (if allowed by your hospital)***

Coach's Bag

camera or video camera with extra batteries*
cash for parking and vending machines*
toiletries, including hairbrush or comb, toothbrush, tooth-
    paste, and deodorant*
bathing suit, if you're planning a water birth**
clothing, two changes**
reading material**
snacks**
something to sleep in**

Postpartum Bag

breast pads*
comfortable going-home outfit*
maternity underwear*
nightgown*
nursing bra, if nursing*
snacks*

list of family and friends to notify when the baby has
 been born**
prepaid calling card**
baby book or journal***
cosmetics***

For Baby

infant car seat*
knit cap*
receiving blanket*
seasonal going-home outfit*
socks or booties*
infant emery board**

*Necessities
**Recommended
***Niceties

What *Not* to Take to the Hospital

checkbook
jewelry
valuables

Hospital Packing Tips

• Since most hospitals won't allow you to eat or drink
 while in active labor, bring hard candies and lip balm
 to help keep your mouth moist.
• Purchase travel-size toiletries so that you can pack
 everything in advance. This way you won't have
 to remember to grab items from the bathroom while
 you're rushing out the door.

- You won't need your postpartum or baby items until after you've given birth, so pack these items separately from those in your labor bag. This way, you can leave what you don't need in the car for your husband or labor coach to get later. If you don't, you'll have to drag everything with you when you're moved from triage to the labor and birthing room to the recovery room.

- A majority of child passenger safety seats are improperly installed, so to be sure that your infant car seat is installed correctly, visit a car seat inspection station. You can find an inspection station in your area by visiting www.seatcheck.org or by calling toll free 866-SEAT CHECK.

- Keep a waterproof pad in your car. It will come in handy to protect your seat on the ride to the hospital if your water has already broken.

- If you opt to bring pillows to the hospital, use colored pillowcases so yours don't get confused with theirs.

- Load your bags into the car for each of your last few doctor visits. They'll come in handy should your physician decide to admit you into the hospital for monitoring or delivery.

14 Questions to Ask before Choosing a Pediatrician

Interviewing a pediatrician may seem like a silly concept, but when choosing your child's health-care provider, you want to be sure that neither your personalities nor your parenting philosophies clash.

Whether you hear about a pediatrician through word of mouth or by finding him or her in the local phone book or online, it's important that you take time to call and set up an appointment to meet the doctor during the last trimester of your pregnancy.

Consider asking these questions when interviewing a potential pediatrician:

Are you board certified in pediatrics?

Are you part of a group practice?

Is there a doctor in this practice available on evenings, weekends, and holidays?

What are your views on bed sharing?

What are your recommendations on vaccinations?

Do you encourage breastfeeding?

Do you have a lactation consultant available?

How long are your scheduled patient appointments?

Do you double book patients?

How are calls handled during office hours?

How are calls handled after office hours?

Do you use email correspondence with patients?

Do you have a nurse's or medical advice line?

Do you take my insurance?

Do you make infants wait in the general waiting area?

Do you have same-day sick visits?

How do you stay current with the latest trends and recommended practices?

Do you consider yourself to have a conservative approach with regard to prescribing medications and tests?

How do you handle referrals to specialists?

At which hospitals do you have admitting privileges?

How do you feel about patients seeking second opinions?

How long have you been practicing?

Will my child usually see a doctor or a nurse practitioner?

How many well visits do you schedule in the first 6 months?

How soon after birth will you see my baby?

Ten Things to Look for When Choosing a Pediatrician

1. board certification
2. after-hours coverage
3. a policy of scheduling same-day sick visits
4. admitting privileges at the hospital of your choice
5. acceptance of your health insurance plan
6. office cleanliness
7. separate waiting areas for sick and well kids
8. friendly office staff
9. credentials on display
10. an office floor plan that is easy to navigate when carrying a car seat, holding a child, or pushing a stroller

Check Up

Before committing to a pediatrician, contact the office of your state medical board to confirm the status of the physician's medical license and to ask for any other information they can give you about the physician. Some states will release information for free about disciplinary actions and malpractice payments.

Looking for a Christian Physician?

Contact the Christian Medical and Dental Associations by calling 888-230-2637 or by visiting http://www.cmda.org to locate a Christian physician in your area.

Wondering When to Take Your Child to the Dentist?

Children are usually seen for their first dental examination when they have all of their baby teeth or around eighteen months.

When Will My Baby Get Teeth?

Babies will grow twenty baby teeth (deciduous teeth) during their first two and half years of life. At around age 6, most children start loosing these teeth and their adult teeth take their place.[16]

	Lower	Upper
Central incisors (two front teeth)	5–7 months	6–8 months
Lateral incisors	7–10 months	8–11 months
Cuspids (canines)	16–20 months	16–20 months
First molars	10–16 months	10–16 months
Second molars	20–30 months	20–30 months[17]

15 Spiritual Comfort for Mom-to-Be

Pregnancy is an emotional time and it can be a time of physical, emotional, and spiritual growth for the Christian mother-to-be.

Take time to talk to God about your worries, fears, and excitement and lean on him and his Word for strength. Thank him for what he has done, what he is doing, and what he will complete.

God Has Not Forgotten You or Your Unborn Child!

You can be confident that this child is part of God's will for your life.
In everything give thanks; for this is the will of God in Christ Jesus for you.

1 Thessalonians 5:18 NKJV

Your child is a blessing!
Children are a heritage from the LORD, the fruit of the womb is a reward.

Psalm 127:3 NKJV

God is forming your child.
You formed my inward parts; You covered me in my mother's womb.

Psalm 139:13 NKJV

You don't have to be afraid; you can trust in God.
Whenever I am afraid, I will trust in You.

Psalm 56:3 NKJV

For God has not given us a spirit of fear, but of power and of love and of a sound mind.

2 Timothy 1:7 NKJV

Do not be afraid, Zacharias, for your prayer is heard; and your wife Elizabeth will bear you a son. . . . And you will have joy and gladness.

Luke 1:13–14 NKJV

God will watch over you and your baby during delivery.
Blessed shall be the fruit of your body.

Deuteronomy 28:4 NKJV

You have control over your emotions and your mind through the power of Jesus Christ.
[Bring] every thought into captivity to the obedience of Christ.

2 Corinthians 10:5 NKJV

God knows you and your child intimately.
The very hairs of your head are all numbered.

Matthew 10:30 NKJV

Thus says the LORD, your Redeemer, and He who formed you from the womb: "I am the LORD, who makes all things."

Isaiah 44:24 NKJV

God will give you the rest that you need.
Come to Me, all you who labor and are heavy laden, and I will give you rest.

Matthew 11:28 NKJV

You can be a great and godly parent.
Commit to the LORD whatever you do, and your plans will succeed.

Proverbs 16:3

God will give you the love and wisdom you need for your child.
Do not provoke your children to wrath, but bring them up in the training and admonition of the Lord.

Ephesians 6:4 NKJV

Christian Parenting

Pregnancy is a great time to focus on the importance of you, your child's, and your family's spirituality.

How will you incorporate your Christian values and principles into your childrearing practices? Will you pray every night as a family? Will you attend church together? It's not too early to begin thinking about these things.

▮▮▮▮ A Month of Prayers for
16 Your Unborn Child

You are probably already praying for good health, safety, and an uncomplicated labor and delivery, but there are other wonderful things you can pray for your child throughout your pregnancy. Bob Hostetler developed this "Parents Prayer Program" and offers thirty-one suggested prayers that parents can pray for their children.[18]

Thirty-one Prayers for Your Unborn Child

1. *Salvation.* "Lord, let salvation spring up within my children, that they 'may obtain the salvation that is in Christ Jesus, with eternal glory'" (Isaiah 45:8; 2 Timothy 2:10).
2. *Growth in grace.* "I pray that they may 'grow in the grace and knowledge of our Lord and Savior Jesus Christ'" (2 Peter 3:18).
3. *Love.* "Grant, Lord, that my children may learn to 'live a life of love,' through the Spirit who dwells in them" (Ephesians 5:2; Galatians 5:22).
4. *Honesty and integrity.* "May 'integrity and honesty' be their virtue and their protection" (Psalm 25:21 NLT).

5. *Self-control.* "Father, help my children not to be like many others around them, but let them be 'alert and self-controlled' in all they do" (1 Thessalonians 5:6).

6. *A love for God's Word.* "May my children grow to find your Word 'more precious than gold, than much pure gold; [and] sweeter than honey, than honey from the comb'" (Psalm 19:10).

7. *Justice.* "God, help my children to love justice as you do and to 'act justly' in all they do" (Psalm 11:7; Micah 6:8).

8. *Mercy.* "May my children always 'be merciful, as [their] Father is merciful'" (Luke 6:36).

9. *Respect (for self, others, authority).* "Father, grant that my children may 'show proper respect to everyone,' as your Word commands" (1 Peter 2:17).

10. *Strong, biblical self-esteem.* "Help my children develop a strong self-esteem that is rooted in the realization that they are 'God's workmanship, created in Christ Jesus'" (Ephesians 2:10).

11. *Faithfulness.* "'Let love and faithfulness never leave [my children],' but bind these twin virtues around their necks and write them on the tablet of their hearts" (Proverbs 3:3).

12. *Courage.* "May my children always 'be strong and courageous' in their character and in their actions" (Deuteronomy 31:6).

13. *Purity.* "'Create in [them] a pure heart, O God,' and let their purity of heart be shown in their actions" (Psalm 51:10).

14. *Kindness.* "Lord, may my children 'always try to be kind to each other and to everyone else'" (1 Thessalonians 5:15).

15. *Generosity.* "Grant that my children may 'be generous and willing to share [and so] lay up treasure for themselves as a firm foundation for the coming age'" (1 Timothy 6:18–19).

16. *Peace, peaceability.* "Father, let my children 'make every effort to do what leads to peace'" (Romans 14:19).
17. *Joy.* "May my children be filled 'with the joy given by the Holy Spirit'" (1 Thessalonians 1:6).
18. *Perseverance.* "Lord, teach my children perseverance in all they do, and help them especially to 'run with perseverance the race marked out for [them]'" (Hebrews 12:1).
19. *Humility.* "God, please cultivate in my children the ability to 'show true humility toward all'" (Titus 3:2).
20. *Compassion.* "Lord, please clothe my children with the virtue of compassion" (Colossians 3:12).
21. *Responsibility.* "Grant that my children may learn responsibility, 'for each one should carry his own load'" (Galatians 6:5).
22. *Contentment.* "Father, teach my children 'the secret of being content in any and every situation . . . through him who gives [them] strength'" (Philippians 4:12–13).
23. *Faith.* "I pray that faith will find root and grow in my children's hearts, that by faith they may gain what has been promised to them" (Luke 17:5–6; Hebrews 11:1–40).
24. *A servant heart.* "God, please help my children develop servant hearts, that they may serve wholeheartedly, 'as to the Lord, and not to men'" (Ephesians 6:7 KJV).
25. *Hope.* "May the God of hope grant that my children may overflow with hope and hopefulness by the power of the Holy Spirit" (Romans 15:13).
26. *The willingness and ability to work hard.* "Teach my children, Lord, to value work and to work hard at everything they do, 'as working for the Lord, not for men'" (Colossians 3:23).
27. *A passion for God.* "Lord, please instill in my children a soul that 'followeth hard after thee,' a heart that clings passionately to you" (Psalm 63:8 KJV).

28. *Self-discipline.* "Father, I pray that my children may develop self-discipline, that they may acquire 'a disciplined and prudent life, doing what is right and just and fair'" (Proverbs 1:3).

29. *Prayerfulness.* "Grant, Lord, that my children's lives may be marked by prayerfulness, that they may learn to 'pray in the Spirit on all occasions with all kinds of prayers and requests'" (Ephesians 6:18).

30. *Gratitude.* "Help my children to live lives that are always 'overflowing with thankfulness,' 'always giving thanks to God the Father for everything, in the name of our Lord Jesus Christ'" (Colossians 2:7; Ephesians 5:20).

31. A *heart for missions.* "Lord, please help my children to develop a heart for missions, a desire to see your glory declared among the nations, your marvelous deeds among all peoples" (Psalm 96:3).

Sons are a heritage from the Lord, children a reward from him.

Psalms 127:3

Before I formed you in the womb I knew you, before you were born I set you apart; I appointed you as a prophet to the nations.

Jeremiah 1:5

God Knows Us Before We Are Born!

For you created my inmost being;
    you knit me together in my mother's womb.
I praise you because I am fearfully and wonderfully made;
    your works are wonderful,
    I know that full well.
My frame was not hidden from you

76

when I was made in the secret place.
When I was woven together in the depths of the
earth,
your eyes saw my unformed body.
All the days ordained for me
were written in your book
before one of them came to be.

Psalm 139:13–16

17 Must-Reads for Mothers-to-Be

It's only natural that during these nine months you want to know *everything* and *anything* about pregnancy, labor, and delivery, but this is one time when the difference between *everything* and *anything* is truly significant. From what changes to expect to managing your nutritional intake to imagining how your child within is progressing week by week—these books will give you the information that you need to make informed decisions and to take charge of your physical and spiritual health.

The Christian Childbirth Handbook by Jennifer Vanderlaan
The Harvard Medical School Guide to Healthy Eating during Pregnancy by W. Allen Walker
Ina May's Guide to Childbirth by Ina May Gaskin
The Nursing Mother's Companion by Kathleen Huggins
What to Expect When You're Expecting by Heidi Murkoff and Sharon Mazel
Working Mom's 411: How to Manage Kids, Career and Home by Michelle LaRowe

Your Pregnancy Devotional: 280 Days of Prayer and Inspiration by Pamela Fierro and Susan Chafin

An Inside Look

If you're wondering exactly what is going on *inside your womb*, I would highly recommend that you check out the National Geographic DVD *In the Womb* (many libraries have copies). From conception to delivery, this DVD uses detailed ultrasonic images and computer animation to track the real-time miracle of life.

LISTS FOR THE FIRST YEAR

18 How Much and How Often Should My Baby Be Eating?

With the growing obesity epidemic in the United States, parents are wondering more than ever just how much their baby should be eating. Unless your baby has unusual special circumstances and your pediatrician has specifically designed a nutritional plan for him, babies should never be on a calorie-restricted diet. The following guidelines can be used as a general reference for feeding healthy, full-term babies.

General Breastfeeding Pattern for the First 6 Months

UNICEF, the American Academy of Pediatrics, and the World Health Organization recommend that infants be breastfed exclusively for the first 6 months of life. At first your baby may spend 10 minutes or more on each breast per feeding. As your baby learns to nurse more effectively, the amount of time he nurses may lessen. You'll know that your baby is getting enough breast milk if she is gaining weight, having several wet diapers throughout the day, and passing runny, seedy, mustard-colored stools after the first 4 or 5 days of life.[1]

Age	Feedings per 24-hour Period
0–1 month	8–12
1–2 months	7–10
2–4 months	6–9
4–6 months	6–8

La Leche League International Breast Milk Storage Guidelines

Breast milk for healthy, full-term infants can be stored in glass, hard-sided plastic BPA free containers with tight fitting lids, or storage bags specifically designed for human milk. Containers should be washed with hot soapy water and allowed to air dry before using. Always wash your hands thoroughly before expressing and storing your milk.

Breast milk may be stored:

- at room temperature (66 to 78°F, 19 to 26°C) for 4 to 6 hours
- in a refrigerator (<39°F, <4°C) for up to 8 days
- in a freezer (–0.4 to –4°F, –18 to –20°C) for up to 12 months

The type of freezer used will affect how long the milk can be safely stored. Milk stored in the back of a separate freezer that doesn't have its door opened frequently will last longer than milk stored in the freezer unit of a refrigerator.[2]

Breast Milk Basics

Don't fill containers to the top. The milk will expand as it freezes and needs room to do so.

Thaw frozen breast milk in the refrigerator or by swirling the container in a bowl of warm water.

Thawed milk can be refrigerated, but should be used within twenty-four hours of defrosting. Do not refreeze thawed breast milk. Stored breast milk may separate. Swirl gently to remix.

Store milk in 2 to 4 ounce portions to minimize waste.

Discard any unused milk once a feeding is complete.

Never warm breast milk in a microwave oven. It may compromise the milk quality or create hot spots that could burn your baby.

Babies may drink breast milk cool, at room temperature, or warmed.

General Guidelines for Average Infant Formula Feeding

To ensure proper growth and development, when babies are fed infant formula, they need to eat daily between 2 and 2.5 ounces of iron-fortified formula per pound of baby's weight.[3]

Age	How Much	Number of Feedings in Twenty-four Hours	Total Amount per Day
1–2 weeks	2–3 fl. oz.	6–10	12–30 fl. oz.
3–4 weeks	3–4 fl. oz.	6–8	18–32 fl. oz.
1–2 months	4–5 fl. oz.	5–6	20–30 fl. oz.
2–3 months	5–6 fl. oz.	5–6	25–36 fl. oz.
3–4 months	6–7 fl. oz.	4–5	24–35 fl. oz.
4–7 months	7–8 fl. oz.	4–5	28–40 fl. oz.
7–9 months	7–8 fl. oz.	3–4	21–32 fl. oz.
9–12 months	7–8 fl. oz.	3	21–24 fl. oz.

Starting Solids

Although the general guideline is to introduce solid foods between 4 to 6 months of age, many pediatricians now recommend waiting until the 6-month mark. See List 20 for information on introducing solid foods to your baby.

19 Breastfeeding Basics

Babies who are breastfed for the first 6 months of life are less likely to experience ear infections, respiratory illnesses, and diarrhea. And the benefits of breastfeeding aren't limited to babies. Mothers who breastfeed their babies have a decreased risk of developing breast and ovarian cancers and tend to have a higher self-esteem.[4] Since breast milk is specifically designed for babies, it meets their nutritional needs perfectly.

Twenty-five Things to Know about Breastfeeding

1. Breastfeeding is a learned art. Give yourself and your baby time to master it.
2. You should try to nurse your baby as soon after birth as possible.
3. Colostrum is the first milk. It is yellowish in color and full of antibodies. Over time your milk will change to a bluish-white color.[5]
4. A mother's milk supply usually comes in on the third or fourth day after giving birth.[6]
5. Healthy, full-term babies nurse, on average, 8–12 times per 24-hour period.[7]
6. Babies may nurse for 10 minutes or more per breast, per feeding.
7. You can tell that your baby is getting enough milk if she has 5 or more wet diapers in a 24-hour period.
8. Breastfed babies usually have mustard-colored, seedy, soft stools, after passing their black, tarlike, and green first stools.

9. The frequency of stools a breastfed baby passes can vary, but on average, breastfed babies have 2–5 soiled diapers per 24-hour period.
10. Some women leak breast milk; others do not. Breast sphincter muscles open and close the milk ducts and keep them from leaking. Breasts do not leak because they are overfull of milk.
11. Breastfed babies should gain on average 4–7 ounces per week after the first 4 days of life.[8]
12. Avoid introducing a pacifier to a breastfeeding baby until nursing is well established.
13. After the first couple of weeks (once your nipples are "toughened up"), breastfeeding should not be painful. Improper latching on by your baby can cause pain.
14. For your baby to latch on properly, be sure her mouth is opened wide and that the nipple is inserted over the tongue, into the back of the baby's mouth. Your baby's lips should be turned out over the areola.
15. You may need to support your breast with your hands while nursing. Grasp your breast behind the areola and cup your hand in the shape of a C to support it.
16. Babies suck and swallow in a distinctive, rhythmic pattern. You should listen for your baby to suck and swallow to be sure that he is latched on properly.
17. To break your baby's latch and release suction, insert your finger into the corner of your baby's mouth.
18. There are several ways to hold your baby while nursing. The most common position is the cradle hold in which your baby's head is cradled in the crook of your arm and her whole body is facing yours, as you gently guide her to your nipple. Another common position is the side lying position. Lie on your side with your baby facing you, and gently pull him to your breast. Often women with large breasts find the football hold most effective for nursing. Hold your baby at your side on her back with her head level to your nipple, supporting

her head with the palm of your hand, and gently guide your baby to your nipple.

19. Women with large breasts, inverted nipples, or more than one baby can successfully breastfeed. You may need a little extra guidance, but it can be done! (Ask about a "nipple guard" if you have inverted nipples. This can be a real help in getting baby to latch on.)

20. Many mothers choose to express their milk and bottle-feed their baby. Hospital-grade breast pumps are best for mothers who opt to express often. Many insurance companies will cover the cost of breast pump rental.

21. Purchasing an AC adapter for your car lighter can make powering your pump and expressing milk on the go convenient and easy.

22. Breastfeeding burns calories—300 to 500 per day![9]

23. Many communities have laws that protect mothers who wish to breastfeed in public. Check your local and state laws to see how you're protected. Nursing covers can help make breastfeeding in public discreet. (Check out "hooter hiders" at www.bebeaulait.com for a fashionable and functional cover that allows you to nurse discreetly.)

24. The American Academy of Pediatrics recommends a supplement of 400 IU per day of vitamin D for all breastfed infants.[10] "Human milk typically contains a vitamin D concentration of 25 IU/L or less. Thus, the recommended adequate intake of vitamin D cannot be met with human milk as the sole source of vitamin D for the breastfeeding infant."[11] Talk to your pediatrician about vitamin D supplements.

25. Certain conditions, like polycystic ovary syndrome, can affect milk supply and production. Talk with your health-care provider about any medical conditions you have that could affect lactation.

Nursing Necessities

two supportive nursing bras
two front-closure sleep bras
two button-up nightgowns or nightshirts
shirts that provide easy access for nursing—most
  women prefer stretchy T-shirt material that can be
  pulled up rather than a buttoned blouse
nipple cream to prevent and treat dry, cracked
  nipples
breast pads

Plus-Size Nursing Gear

Birth and Baby, located in Lind, Washington, has the
best selection of nursing bras for plus-sized women. If
you don't live locally, don't worry. They ship throughout the United States for one dollar and encourage
women to try on as many styles and sizes as they
need to find the right fit. They have a no hassle, no fee
return policy and can even provide a phone fitting to
help you choose the right size. Visit their online stores
at birthandbaby.com and www.birthandbabyorders.
com or call them at 888-398-7987.

20 Introducing Solid Foods

UNICEF, the American Academy of Pediatrics, and the World
Health Organization recommend that infants be breastfed
exclusively for the first 6 months of life. All three organiza-

tions also recommend that breastfeeding continue, with the addition of solid foods, for at least twelve months.[12]

Delaying the introduction of solid foods until your baby is 6 months of age is advised, because before then your baby's intestines may not be mature enough to handle solid foods, her tongue-thrust reflex is still strong, and her swallowing mechanism is still maturing.[13] In addition: "Introducing supplemental foods during the first 4 months of life has been associated with a higher risk for allergic diseases."[14]

Although it used to be thought that babies should be introduced to vegetables before fruit so they don't develop a sweet tooth, the American Academy for Pediatrics debunks that myth, stating that for most infants, the order that foods are introduced does not matter.[15] However, since rice is easy to digest and is gluten free, rice cereal is often the first food recommended.

First Foods for Baby[16]

At 6 Months

Grains: vitamin-fortified cereal
Vegetables: acorn squash, butternut squash, peas, and sweet potatoes
Fruits: apples, bananas, and pears

Between 6 and 8 Months

Grains: vitamin-fortified cereal
Vegetables: add pumpkin, yellow squash, zucchini
Fruits: avocados, apricots, nectarines, peaches, and plums
Protein: chicken, tofu, and turkey

Between 8 and 10 Months

Grains: whole-grain O-shaped cereals
Vegetables: carrots, cauliflower, green beans, spinach, sugar snap peas
Fruits: quartered grapes, mango, and papaya
Protein: beans
Dairy: yogurt and cheese made from whole milk[17]

Between 10 and 12 Months

Grains: egg-free pasta
Vegetables: eggplant, cucumber, and white potatoes
Fruits: blueberries
Protein: egg yolks and lamb

Forbidden Foods for Baby

Never feed the following foods to babies who are 1 year or younger. Introducing these foods poses allergy and health risks.[18]

corn
corn syrup
egg whites
honey
peanut butter
shellfish
strawberries
tree nuts
whole milk (excludes yogurt and cheese)

Tips for Introducing Solid Foods

Introduce your baby to one new food at a time. Wait at least five days between introducing new foods to your baby so you can monitor your child for allergic reactions.

Introduce rice cereal first, followed by oatmeal, then barley. Wheat cereals should be introduced last.

Introduce single-ingredient foods first; then try combination foods. For example, give mixed-grain cereals after your baby has tried a variety of single-grain cereals.

How to Make Your Own Baby Food

1. Steam or bake fresh fruits or vegetables until tender.
2. Puree cooked fruits or vegetables in a food processor or blender.
3. Fill an ice cube tray with pureed food.
4. Cover the filled ice cube tray with plastic wrap and freeze.
5. Once the puree cubes are frozen, transfer them to a plastic freezer storage bag and label it with the food type and date. Cubes should be used within one month of freezing.
6. Thaw and heat as needed. Breast milk, formula, or water can be added to thin the puree before serving. Each cube equals about 1 ounce of baby food.

⧠⧠⧠⧠ Length and Weight Guidelines
21 for the First Year

Although all babies develop at different rates, during the first year you can expect your baby to:

- gain on average 4–7 ounces per week for the first month
- gain on average 1–2 pounds per month for the first 6 months
- gain on average 1 pound per month from 6 months to 1 year of age
- grow on average 1 inch per month for the first 6 months
- grow on average ½ inch per month from 6 months to 1 year[19]

Breastfed babies and formula fed babies develop at slightly different rates. At the end of 12 months, on average, breastfed babies gain 1 pound less than formula fed babies.[20]

An average loss of 5 to 7 percent of body weight during the first few days of life is normal.[21] Babies usually regain lost weight and reach or exceed their birth weight by 2 weeks of age.[22]

Standard growth charts based on percentiles are commonly used to monitor and assess the growth and development of babies and children. "Percentiles rank the position of an individual by indicating what percent of the reference population the individual would equal or exceed. For example, on the weight-for-age growth charts, a

91

Birth to 36 months: Boys
Length-for-age and Weight-for-age percentiles

NAME _____

RECORD # _____

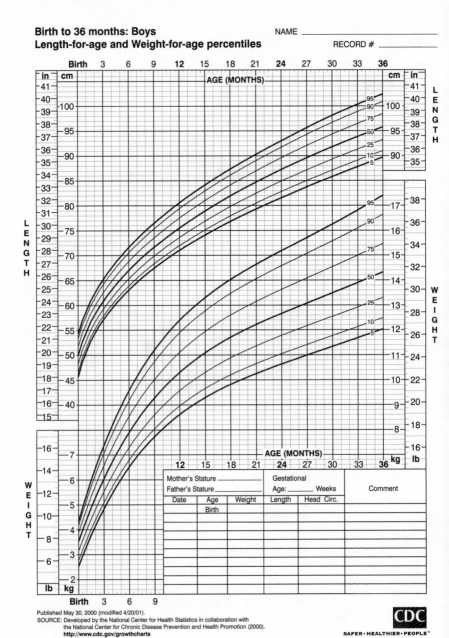

Published May 30, 2000 (modified 4/20/01).
SOURCE: Developed by the National Center for Health Statistics in collaboration with
the National Center for Chronic Disease Prevention and Health Promotion (2000).
http://www.cdc.gov/growthcharts

CDC
SAFER · HEALTHIER · PEOPLE™

Birth to 36 months: Girls
Length-for-age and Weight-for-age percentiles

NAME _____

RECORD # _____

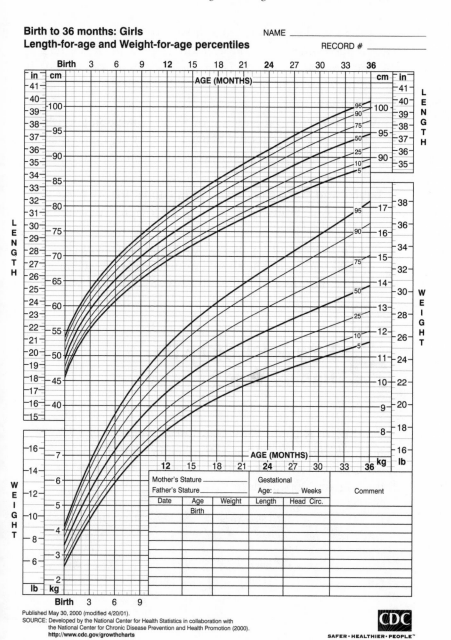

Published May 30, 2000 (modified 4/20/01).
SOURCE: Developed by the National Center for Health Statistics in collaboration with
the National Center for Chronic Disease Prevention and Health Promotion (2000).
http://www.cdc.gov/growthcharts

CDC
SAFER · HEALTHIER · PEOPLE™

5-year-old girl whose weight is at the 25th percentile, weighs the same or more than 25 percent of the reference population of 5-year-old girls, and weighs less than 75 percent of the 5-year-old girls in the reference population."[23]

When monitoring a baby's growth and development, it's important to focus on the change in growth, rather than on the numbers or on the percentile at which your baby falls.

Babies who fail to gain weight or fall under the 5th percentile may be evaluated by their pediatrician to determine why.

If your baby is following his curve on the growth chart, you'll notice that he should double his birth weight in 4 to 6 months and triple it by 1 year.

22 How Much Sleep Do Babies Need?

According to Richard Ferber, author of *Solve Your Child's Sleep Problems* and director of the Center for Pediatric Sleep Disorders at Boston's Children's Hospital, babies need the following amounts of sleep:[24]

Age	Total Sleep (typical)	Nighttime Sleep	Daytime Sleep
Full-term newborn	16 hours	varies	varies
3 months	13 hours	8.5 hours	4.5 hours
6 months	12.5 hours	9.25 hours	3.25 hours
1 year	11.75 hours	9.75 hours	2 hours

Sleeping Soundly

Babies are born nocturnal. To help babies switch their internal clock, create a dark, soothing atmosphere for nighttime sleep. During morning and midday snoozes, don't close the shades or keep things extra quiet. You want your baby to associate "light" with daytime stimulation and "dark" with uninterrupted nighttime sleep.

You can begin to put your baby on a sleep schedule when she is around three months of age. By five months, most healthy, full-term babies should be sleeping though the night, although some will sleep through much sooner and others much later.

Never use blankets in a baby's crib or bassinet. Instead, invest in a good swaddling blanket, sleep sack, or wearable blanket. Sleep sacks give your baby the warmth she needs and eliminates the risk of getting caught up and suffocating in a loose blanket. Swaddling helps to maximize your baby's sleep, and baby wraps make swaddling easy.[25]

SIDS

The American Academy of Pediatrics makes the following recommendations for reducing the risk of SIDS (sudden infant death syndrome):[26]

Always put your baby to sleep on her back.

Use a firm sleep surface.

Keep soft objects and loose bedding out of the crib.

Do not smoke during pregnancy.

Use a separate sleep space for your baby that is close to you. A bassinet in your room or a co-sleeper that attaches to your bed works best.

Consider using a pacifier during sleep time.

Avoid overdressing your baby. Use lightweight sleepwear and keep the bedroom at a temperature that is comfortable for a lightly dressed adult.

Don't use commercial devices (such as sleep positioners) marketed to reduce SIDS, as they haven't been tested enough to determine their effectiveness or safety.

Don't use home monitors as a strategy to reduce the risk of SIDS, as there is no evidence that they decrease the incidence of SIDS.

Do use a fan in your infant's room. A 2008 study published in the Archives of Pediatric & Adolescent Medicine found that using a fan in an infant's room during sleep was associated with a 72 percent reduction in SIDS risk.[27]

Avoid development of positional plagiocephaly (flattened head) by encouraging tummy time, avoiding long periods of time in bouncers or car seat carriers and by altering the side of the head that your baby sleeps on, as well as periodically changing his or her orientation to the room.

Sleep Tip

Avoid putting your baby to bed with a bottle or cup. Fluids can pool in your baby's mouth and cause tooth decay. When a baby is lying flat while drinking, fluids can also enter the eustatian tubes of the ears and cause an ear infection.[28]

23 Sleep Training Your Baby

It's every parent's dream to have a baby that sleeps through the night, and for parents who choose to sleep train their babies, that dream isn't a farfetched one. As a mother (whose baby has slept through the night since she was five weeks and three days old!) and as a nanny, I can tell you with great assurance that babies who have good sleep habits are less fussy, are more content, and grow into toddlers who have less frequent meltdowns.

The Mindset for Sleep Training Your Baby

Understand that learning to fall asleep on your own and getting yourself back to sleep after waking up are life skills that your baby can master.

Understand that rocking your baby to sleep or allowing him to fall asleep while feeding inhibits him from learning to fall asleep on his own.

Understand that crying is part of the process. As your baby learns to master this new skill, tears are inevitable.

Understand that your baby is able to sleep through the night when he is physically and emotionally ready. Most babies are ready between 4 to 6 months of age.

The Process for Sleep Training Your Baby

Dr. Richard Ferber developed an excellent sleep training method. [29] Here is a simplified version:

1. Put your baby into his crib when he is drowsy but still awake.
2. Say good night to your baby, shut off the lights, and leave the room.
3. If your baby cries, allow him to cry for a predetermined amount of time. Start off by letting him cry for three minutes.
4. Go back into the room and gently reassure him that you are there by speaking softly and patting him on the back. Do not turn on the lights and do not pick up your baby. Leave the room while he is still awake.
5. Keep repeating step 4, gradually increasing the amount of time that you wait to go into his room until he falls asleep while you are out of the room.
6. If your baby wakes during the night, repeat steps 4 and 5.
7. Each night increase the interval of time before going back into the baby's room.
8. Expect your baby to learn to go to sleep on his own in less than a week.

Nightly Visits

Night of Training	Visit to Nursery	Minutes between Visits
1	1st	3
1	2nd	5
1	3rd and more	10
2	1st	5
2	2nd	10
2	3rd and more	12
3	1st	10
3	2nd	12
3	3rd and more	15

Sleep Training Tips for Success

- Establish a bedtime routine. Babies feel safe and secure when they know what to expect next. A bath, a book, and a big hug at the same time, in the same order, each night is the simplest of bedtime routines.

- Make a plan and stick to it. If you and your spouse aren't equally committed to following through with a sleep training plan, it's not going to work.
- Prepare for a few nights of fussing. Expect your baby to fuss for the first few nights as he becomes adjusted to learning to fall asleep on his own.
- Remember that if your baby's needs are met, it can be easier to handle the crying. If you know that your baby is healthy, fed, changed, and in a safe and secure sleeping environment, you can be comforted and confident in letting him learn to fall asleep on his own.
- Although this approach is often called the "cry it out" method, crying isn't the goal, it's a side effect of the process.
- If your baby is sick, be sure to give him all the attention and comfort he needs and take a break from the sleep training.

Sleep Soundly

Having white noise in your baby's background can help promote sleep. Keep a fan on or purchase a sound machine to create soothing sounds for your baby to sleep to (like the Obus Forme Sound Machine, available at amazon.com).

24 Developmental Milestones for the First Year

It's normal to wonder if your baby is growing and developing on track. While every child grows and develops at his or her own pace, there are some benchmark milestones that most children reach during their first year. The following is a checklist of widely accepted, standard developmental milestones you can expect healthy, full-term babies to achieve. Most parenting resources will include these basic benchmarks for helping you to evaluate your baby's development.

By the End of 3 Months

Physical

Most children can:

- ✓ lift their head when you are holding them on your shoulder
- ✓ lift their head and chest when lying on their stomach
- ✓ turn their head from side to side when lying on their stomach
- ✓ follow moving objects and people with their eyes
- ✓ hold hands open or in a loose fist
- ✓ grasp a small rattle when it is given to them
- ✓ wiggle arms and kick legs

Intellectual

Most children can:

✓ turn their head to look at bright and bold colors
✓ turn their head to look for the owner of a voice
✓ recognize feeding time by the bottle or the breast

Social and Emotional

Most children can:

✓ smile socially
✓ make cooing and gurgling sounds
✓ communicate hunger, discomfort, and fear through crying and facial expressions
✓ calm when hearing a familiar voice or seeing a familiar face
✓ anticipate being picked up
✓ react to smiles and voices

By the End of 6 Months

Physical

Most children can:

✓ hold their head steady when sitting with your assistance
✓ reach for objects
✓ grasp objects
✓ play with toes
✓ help hold their bottle during feeding
✓ transfer toys from one hand to the other
✓ shake a rattle
✓ pull up to a sitting position if you grasp their hands
✓ roll over (babies usually roll from their tummy to back first)

✓ bounce when standing with your help

Intellectual

Most children can:

✓ imitate things you do
✓ open their mouth for a spoon

Social and Emotional

Most children can:

✓ babble
✓ recognize familiar faces
✓ laugh
✓ squeal when excited or happy
✓ scream if irritated or annoyed
✓ smile at self in a mirror

By the Age of 12 Months

Physical

Most children can:

✓ drink from a sippy cup with help
✓ feed themselves small finger foods
✓ use pincer grasp to pick up small objects
✓ use first finger to point
✓ bang two blocks together
✓ sit without support
✓ crawl
✓ pull to standing
✓ cruise around furniture

✓ walk with one hand held
✓ cooperate when getting dressed by offering a hand or foot

Intellectual

Most children can:

✓ copy sounds and actions
✓ respond to music
✓ crawl to get a toy or desired object
✓ look for something that they've dropped

Social and Emotional

Most children can:

✓ babble in a way that sounds like talking or singing
✓ say their first word
✓ recognize the names of family members
✓ respond to someone's crying by crying
✓ show apprehension with strangers
✓ raise arms to signal "pick me up"
✓ understand simple commands

A Note about Preemies

Developmental milestones for preemies are based on their adjusted age. If your baby is 5 months old and was born 2 months early, for example, use his adjusted age of 3 months to gauge his growth and development.

Don't Compare!

Resist the urge to compare your child to others. Each child develops on her own timeline. When gauging *your child's development, it's important to observe her over the course of a few weeks to get an accurate picture of her developmental level. If you are concerned that your child isn't reaching these milestones at the appropriate age, talk to your child's pediatrician.*

25 Top Toys for the First Year

For Babies under 6 Months

Toys for babies under 6 months of age should be geared toward sensory and motor development. Both black and white and bright and bold colored objects will greatly interest your baby during this stage of development. Once your baby begins to grab at objects or mouth them, textured toys are a great choice.

activity quilts
cloth or board books
interactive play mats
mobiles with lights and motion
musical toys
music tapes or CDs
plastic links
plush toys that make noise
rattles
soft balls
soft blocks
teething rings and toys
textured balls and toys
unbreakable mirrors

For Babies 6–12 Months

Toys for babies 6 to 12 months of age should be geared toward interactive play. Toys that show cause and effect and promote hand-eye coordination are great for this stage of development. Anything that makes noise or that can be banged, dropped, stacked, piled up, knocked over, or opened and shut will greatly interest your baby.

bath toys
cloth or board books
doorway jumper or
   saucer
musical instruments
musical toys
music tapes or CDs
nesting cups
plastic cell phone
plastic child-safe keys
plastic photo album

plush toys that vibrate
pop-up toys
pull toys
push toys that make
   noise
shape sorters
soft blocks
stacking toys
stuffed animals, dolls,
   and toys

Playing Is Learning

When it comes to babies, toys have a greater purpose than just entertainment. Playing is your baby's primary mode for learning and development. For this reason, choosing stimulating, age-appropriate toys is important to foster your baby's cognitive, physical, and social development.

Safety First

To prevent injury and strangulation, remove mobiles when your baby is able to push up on his hands and knees. Never attach strings to toys, cribs, strollers, or infant seats.

Make Time for Tummy Time

Because moms are encouraged to put their babies to sleep on their backs, it's important to incorporate tummy time into each day to promote proper muscle development and to keep your baby's head from getting flat spots. Play mats or activity quilts make great tummy time toys.

26 What Goes in My Diaper Bag?

Being prepared, especially when on the go, is one of the keys to successful parenting. If you use the following list to pack your diaper bag, you'll be prepared for almost anything!

baby food
baby spoon
Band-aids
bib
blanket
bottled water
bottles
burp cloth
change of clothes
changing pad
diaper rash cream
diapers
emergency information
fever reducer
formula

hand sanitizer
hat
lotion
nursing cover
nursing pads
pacifier
plastic bags to hold
    soiled clothes or
    diapers
small toys
sunscreen
thermometer
tissues
Vaseline
wet wipes

Diaper Bag Dos

Do restock your diaper bag immediately after each use.

Do remove soiled clothing and diapers as soon as you return home.

Do remember to update your spare clothes as your baby grows and as the seasons change.

Do clean your diaper bag thoroughly at least once per month.

Do have a spare diaper bag packed that you can easily grab if you're in a rush.

Do keep a small diaper bag with changing and feeding necessities in the car.

Do consider leaving a fully stocked diaper bag in the car and toting a smaller bag that holds just changing and feeding necessities with you.

Diaper Bag Don'ts

Don't hang your diaper bag on the handles of your stroller, unless it's meant to go there. The uneven distribution of weight can cause your stroller to tip over and injure your child.

Don't leave a diaper bag with prepared formula in the car overnight. Extreme heat and cold can compromise the quality of the formula.

Don't choose a diaper bag that can't be easily wiped clean. If it's difficult to clean and formula gets into its nooks and crannies, it will smell stinky.

Tips for Choosing a Diaper Bag

Your diaper bag will get years of use, so when choosing a diaper bag be sure to look for one that is made of a durable, washable fabric. You'll also want to choose a diaper bag that is well constructed and has good quality stitching and heavy-duty zippers. When making your selection, look for additional features such as adjustable straps, an oversized changing pad, a coordinating insulated bag, and lots of compartments and pockets. Many moms enjoy the backpack model of diaper bags, which allows their hands to be free. My personal favorite is the Glazed Boxy Backpack from Petunuia Pickle Bottom (petuniapicklebottom.com).

27 Traveling with Baby

Traveling with a baby requires careful planning and packing and there's no better way to keep track of what you need and what you're bringing than a detailed list. Use this list as a guide to plan and pack for your travel adventure with baby.

Health and Hygiene

	Bring	Ship	Buy
diapers	☐	☐	☐
wipes	☐	☐	☐
changing pad	☐	☐	☐
diaper rash cream	☐	☐	☐
body wash	☐	☐	☐
lotion	☐	☐	☐
toothbrush	☐	☐	☐
toothpaste	☐	☐	☐

hairbrush	☐	☐	☐
washcloths	☐	☐	☐
baby towel	☐	☐	☐
pain reliever	☐	☐	☐
medications	☐	☐	☐
laundry detergent	☐	☐	☐
hand sanitizer	☐	☐	☐

Clothing

Record the number of items you are packing on each line.

_____ long-sleeved shirts

_____ short-sleeved shorts

_____ pants

_____ shorts

_____ skirts

_____ short-sleeved snap T-shirts

_____ long-sleeved snap T-shirts

_____ sleepwear

_____ one-piece outfits

_____ dress outfits

_____ socks

_____ shoes

_____ tights

_____ hats

_____ swimwear

_____ jacket/sweater

_____ snowsuit

_____ mittens

_____ boots

Gear

	Bring	Rent	Borrow	Ship
car seat	☐	☐	☐	☐
stroller	☐	☐	☐	☐
carrier	☐	☐	☐	☐
high chair	☐	☐	☐	☐
sleep space	☐	☐	☐	☐
toys	☐	☐	☐	☐

Feeding

☐ bottles
☐ nipples
☐ formula
☐ baby utensils
☐ breast pump
☐ milk storage supplies
☐ dish soap

☐ snacks
☐ baby food
☐ bottled water
☐ juice boxes
☐ bibs
☐ burp cloths
☐ sippy cups

Safety

☐ childproofing items
☐ night-light
☐ first aid kit

☐ sunscreen
☐ bug spray

Miscellaneous

Record the number of items you are packing on each line.

_____ swaddle blankets
_____ wearable blanket

_____ plastic bags for soiled clothing and diapers
_____ favorite toys
_____ books
_____ music CDs
_____ comfort items
_____ pacifiers
_____ camera
_____ camera accessories
_____ emergency contact information

Traveling Tips

- *Research your destination.* Know what your living space will be like and what gear may be available for you to use on arrival.
- *Research your travel options.* You'll want to know if the airline offers discounts or free fare for babies, and if your car rental company offers complimentary safety seats.
- *Consider shipping or borrowing at your destination* some of the things that you'll need. This can save you a bundle if you're flying.
- *Consider buying consumable goods on location.* This can save space when traveling by car and money if traveling by plane.
- *Keep handy a change of clothes for yourself.* You don't want to be stuck shuffling through luggage to find a spare shirt if you've been spit up on.
- *Many popular travel destinations are home to companies that rent baby gear, including toys.* Check with your hotel, resort, or the chamber of commerce where you are visiting to see if there is a baby rental store in the area.
- *Bring your packing list with you* so that you can be sure to come home with everything you took with you.

Formula Formulations

Individual bottles of ready-made formula are the most convenient for traveling, but if they are out of your price range, consider purchasing the less expensive individual tubes of formula powder that can be added to water and mixed directly in a bottle. An even less expensive option: purchase divided plastic containers that store premeasured amounts of formula from the baby section of your local department store.

28 The Best Baby Gear

Having the right gear can make bringing home baby a whole lot easier and these two dozen mommy must-haves are guaranteed to make the practicalities of parenting during the first year much more manageable.

1. bassinet or co-sleeper that attaches to the side of your bed
2. infant car seat with two bases
3. bunting bag for the car seat and stroller
4. stroller frame for your infant car seat
5. good quality umbrella stroller with a reclining seat
6. convertible car seat
7. hospital-quality breast pump
8. nursing pillow
9. nursing cover
10. bottles with disposable liners
11. infant wrap for swaddling
12. assortment of side-snap shirts

13. resealable packages of wet wipes
14. diaper pail that uses any plastic bag
15. infant bathtub or bathing seat
16. assortment of cloth diapers
17. assortment of waterproof changing pads
18. waterproof, easy to change crib sheet that snaps or zips on
19. baby monitor
20. bouncy seat or infant chair
21. high chair that has a reclining seat
22. portable travel chair that attaches to a table
23. large, compartmentalized, washable diaper bag
24. portable play yard

Top Picks

Arm's Reach Mini Co-Sleeper

Practical, portable, and space-saving, the Mini Co-Sleeper allows parents to sleep safely beside their babies. A great and safe alternative to bed sharing, this bassinet attaches to the side of your bed, allowing your baby to sleep at the same height as you in her own safe and secure space. The Arm's Reach Mini Co-Sleeper puts your baby literally within arms reach for easy night feedings and comforting. This co-sleeper is especially useful for mothers recovering from a cesarean section or mothers who are breastfeeding (http://www.armsreach.com/).

Baby Cozy's World Microfiber and Fleece Infant Car Seat Carrier Cover

One of the best baby inventions ever, the Baby Cozy's Car Seat Carrier Cover keeps your baby warm without interfering with the harness system of the infant car seat carrier. Simply slide the sleeping bag like cover

over the car seat and your baby will be snug as a bug in a rug, literally. No more bulky winter jackets or chasing stray baby blankets with this mommy must-have. The Baby Cozy is available from Target stores, Target.com, and Amazon.com.

Maclaren Techno Buggy

With a five-point harness, a four position seat that can fully recline, and an extendable leg rest (allowing for comfy naps), the Maclaren Techno Buggy is designed for parents on the go. It's easy to maneuver this stroller in and out of stores, and with its one-hand umbrella style fold, it can fit into the trunk of any vehicle. The stroller is designed for newborns to children up to 55 pounds, so if you want to buy only one stroller, this is it. The seat is completely washable, and the company offers a lifetime warranty. Maclaren also makes a double buggy that is just as perfect (http://www.maclarenbaby.com/).

Berkley and Jensen Baby Unscented Ultra Soft Cloths Solo Pack

This pack of wet wipes is a soft package with a flip top that stays shut, which makes for easy tossing into a diaper bag and means the wipes don't dry out. It comes with eighty quilted wipes and is a great alternative to the more commonly used plastic refillable storage boxes that never seem to hold enough.

■■■ Twenty-five Things You Think
29 You Really Need but Really Don't

It can be very tempting to buy your baby everything, and if you've spent time perusing the baby aisles, you've already discovered that there is literally something for everything. Don't buy into the gizmos and marketing gimmicks. Here are twenty-five things you can definitely live without.

1. *A bottle warmer.* Save money and instead heat your bottles by placing them in a cup of warm water.
2. *A wipes warmer.* Wipes stored at room temperature are perfectly fine for baby.
3. *A bottle sterilizer.* Place bottles on the top rack of the dishwasher or in boiling water for 5 to 10 minutes to sterilize.
4. *Bottle proppers.* Never use anything to prop your baby's bottle. It can put your baby at a risk of aspirating the milk.
5. *A mirror for the car.* A mirror can be distracting and dangerous if it were to come loose in an accident.
6. *Car seat headrests.* Avoid accessories that did not come with the car seat. They can impact your car seat's integrity and may even void your warranty.
7. *Crib bumpers.* Avoid using fluffy crib bumpers. They can pose suffocation and strangulation risks to infants. If you feel bumpers are necessary, opt for ones made of mesh material.
8. *Plush blankets.* Babies should never be put to bed with loose blankets. They can pose suffocation and strangulation risks. Instead, opt for wearable baby blankets.

115

9. *Pillows.* Babies should not use pillows; they pose a suffocation risk.

10. *SIDS prevention devices.* The American Academy of Pediatrics recommends not using home devices marketed to reduce the risk of SIDS. Their effectiveness has not been tested.

11. *A sleep positioner.* These are soft and plush and should not be placed in cribs because they pose a suffocation risk.

12. *A diaper pail that requires special bags.* To save money, select a pail that accepts any plastic bag.

13. *Pee-pee tents.* Do these need an explanation?

14. *A changing table.* Save money by placing a changing pad on the floor, on the bed, or on top of a wide, flat surface when changing your baby.

15. *A scale.* Unless your pediatrician specifically recommends that you have one at home, save the weigh-ins for your child's doctor appointments.

16. *A robe.* A hooded towel works just fine for wrapping and warming baby and the robe belt can pose a strangulation hazard.

17. *A shopping cart and high chair cover.* With these products, you'll end up bringing home more germs than you left with. Instead, wipe down surfaces with antibacterial wipes.

18. *Knee pads.* Bumps, bruises, and scratches are part of the daily life of a toddler. If they bother you, dress your baby in pants.

19. *Toddler or "transitional" formulas.* Unless your pediatrician specifically prescribes them, they aren't necessary. By the age of one, children should be getting all of their nutrients from nutritious meals, snacks, and drinks.

20. *A baby leash.* A better option than a leash is your hand. Teach your young children to walk next to you and if they refuse, put them into a stroller.

21. *Shoes.* Babies need to be barefoot so they can feel and grip the surface as they learn to walk. Shoes are needed only to provide protection from hot, hard, or rough surfaces. Be sure baby's first shoes are soft and flexible so that your baby can have full range of foot motion. Robeez (www.robeez.com) and See Kai Run (www.seekairun.com) are makers of great first shoes.
22. *Baby life insurance.* The only advantage to purchasing baby life insurance is that it usually comes with a guarantee that your baby will always be eligible for coverage, but the amount that the policy would pay out usually isn't enough to make it worth the premiums.
23. *Perfumed lotions and oils.* These can be harsh on a baby's delicate skin and the fragrances may irritate your baby. Instead, choose an all-natural hypoallergenic baby wash.
24. *Sprays to clean pacifiers.* Although there may be a few places where you won't have access to a sink, it's better to hold out. Soap and water is probably best for baby.
25. *Baby headbands.* Cute as can be, but they pose a strangulation risk to babies.

Top Five Baby Products You Can't Live Without

While a crib, diapers, and wipes are no-brainers, here are five other must-have items.

1. *A co-sleeping bassinet.* Provides a separate, safe, and secure sleep space for your baby that attaches to your bed. Top pick: Arm's Reach Mini-Co Sleeper (http://www.armsreach.com/).
2. *A stroller frame to accommodate your infant car seat.* Makes going out and about with baby a breeze. Top pick: Uppa Baby Vista (www.uppababy.com).

3. *An infant wrap.* Makes swaddling super easy and keeps baby super snug. Top pick: Kiddopotamus Bamboo SwaddleMe (www.kiddopotamus.com/).

4. *An infant car seat with base.* You won't need to fuss with belt buckles once the base is securely fastened into the vehicle. You'll just snap the seat into and out of the base. Top pick: Graco SnugRide (www.gracobaby.com).

5. *Sheet savers.* Place a soft, waterproof sheet securely over the crib mattress to make middle of the night sheet changes simple. Top pick: Basic Comfort Ultimate Crib Sheet (www.summerinfant.com).

30 Must-Haves for Multiples

Managing multiples becomes a whole lot easier if you have the right equipment. The following is a list of items that make parenting two or more much more manageable.

backpack-style diaper bag to keep your hands free when out

double stroller frame for two infant car seats

infant carrier so you can hold one twin hands-free

notebook to keep track of your twins' feedings and elimination

nursing pillow to support your twins while feeding

play yard to use for sleeping and as a safe place to keep your twins

reclining double stroller to easily transport your twins while out and about

subscription to *TWINS* magazine

Things You'll Need Two Of

When it comes to multiples, you don't really need two of everything, but there are some items that you'll have to double up on.

bouncing seats	high chairs
car seat bunting bags	swings
cribs	

Top Picks

Double Decker Stroller

The Double Decker Stroller is a lightweight frame that fits two infant car seats in tandem fashion with one sitting above the other. It makes transporting twins super easy. The Double Decker folds compactly and can fit into the trunk of most vehicles. There is also a Triple Decker Stroller (www.doubledeckerstroller.com).

Affordable alternative: Baby Trend Double Snap and Go Stroller Frame (www.babytrend.com).

Friendly Toys Little Playzone with Lights and Sound

You'll definitely need a safe place to put your twins when you run to the bathroom or cook dinner. This play yard provides thirteen square feet of play space that you can make even bigger by purchasing expansion panels. With colorful panels and toys attached for play, just line the bottom with foam matting and you have an instant safe and secure play area for your multiples (www.toysrus.com).

Affordable alternative: North States Superyard XT Gate Play Yard (www.northstatesind.com).

Maclaren Twin Techno Buggy

The Twin Techno Buggy has dual, side-by-side independently reclining seats and expanding leg rests, making it perfect for naps. It is suitable for babies from birth to 55 pounds. Swivel wheels make it easy to maneuver and it is narrow enough to fit through a standard doorway. Its lightweight umbrella style fold makes it easy to fold and fit into the trunk of any vehicle (www.maclarenbaby.com).

Affordable alternative: Jeep Wrangler Twin Sport All Weather (available at amazon.com).

Graco Pack 'n' Play with Twins Bassinet

This is two bassinets, providing a space-saving alternative for your twins to sleep during the first months. When your twins are older, you can use the pack and play as a spare sleep space when traveling or to separate your twins during naptime (www.gracobaby.com).

Affordable alternative: Evenflo BabySuite Classic Play Yard (www.evenflo.com).

By the Numbers

In the first two months, parents of twins will:

- change 16 to 24 diapers each day
- use 960 to 1,440 disposable diapers
- feed each twin 8 times per 24-hour period
- wash 992 bottles
- use 2,000–3,000 wipes
- use 2,108–3,968 ounces of formula

31 Lyrics to Twenty-two Traditional Nursery Rhymes and Songs

Nursery rhymes are traditional poems and songs that were taught to young children to help them with counting, vocabulary, learning morals and life principles, and following directions. Usually passed down by oral tradition from generation to generation, many of these rhymes had historical, political, violent, or dangerous undertones and were often used as a means to spread rebellious messages.[30] If you'd like to teach your child some of the more innocent rhymes, try passing down these classics.

A B C Tumble

A, B, C, tumble down D,
The cat's in the cupboard
And can't see me.

A-Hunting We Will Go

A-hunting we will go,
A-hunting we will go,
We'll catch a fox
And put him in a box
And then we'll let him go.

A-Tisket, a-Tasket

A-tisket, a-tasket,
A green and yellow basket.
I wrote a letter to my love,
But on the way I dropped it.
I dropped it, I dropped it,
And, on the way I dropped it.
A little boy picked it up,
And put it in his pocket.

121

Dance Baby

Dance little baby, dance up high,
Never mind, baby, mother is by;
Crow and caper, caper and crow,
There, little baby, there you go.
Up to the ceiling, down to the ground,
Backwards and forwards, round and round;
Dance, little baby, and mother will sing
With the merry coral, ding, ding, ding!

Dance to Your Daddy

Dance to your daddy, my little laddie
Dance to your daddy, my little man
Thou should have a fish and thou should have a fin
Thou should have a cuddling when the boat comes in
Thou should have a haddock baked in a pan
Dance to your daddy, my little man
Dance to your daddy, my little laddie
Dance to your daddy, my little man
When thou art a man and come to take a wife
Thou should wed a lass and love her all your life
She should be your lass and thou should be her man
Dance to your daddy, my little man

Do Re Mi

Doe, a deer, a female deer
Ray, a drop of golden sun
Me, a name I call myself
Far, a long, long way to run
Sew, a needle pulling thread
La, a note to follow sew
Tea, I drink with jam and bread
That will bring us back to
Do re mi fa so la ti do, so, do!

Early to Bed

Early to bed,
Early to rise.

Makes little Johnny,
Healthy, wealthy, and wise.

Eeny Meeny Miny Mo

Eeny, meeny, miny, mo,
Catch a tiger by the toe:
If he hollers let him go,
Eeny, meeny, miny, mo.

Fingers and Toes

Every lady in this land
Has twenty nails upon each hand,
Five and twenty on hands and feet:
All this is true, without deceit.

Five Little Ducks

Five little ducks went swimming one day,
Over the hill and far away.
Mother duck said, "Quack, quack, quack,"
And only four little ducks came back.
Four little ducks went swimming one day,
Over the hill and far away.
Mother duck said, "Quack, quack, quack,"
And only three little ducks came back.
Three little ducks went swimming one day,
Over the hill and far away.
Mother duck said, "Quack, quack, quack,"
And only two little ducks came back.
Two little ducks went swimming one day,
Over the hill and far away.
Mother duck said, "Quack, quack, quack,"
And only one little duck came back.
One little duck went swimming one day,
Over the hill and far away.
Mother duck said, "Quack, quack, quack,"
And five little ducks came back.

Head, Shoulders, Knees, and Toes

Head, shoulders, knees, and toes,
Knees and toes,

Head, shoulders, knees, and toes,
Knees and toes,
Eyes and ears and mouth and nose,
Head, shoulders, knees, and toes,
Knees and toes.

Here Is the Church

Here is the church, and here is the steeple.
Open the door and see all the people.
Here is the parson going upstairs,
And here he is, saying his prayers.

Here We Go Loop de Loop

Here we go loop de loop
Here we go loop de lie
Here we go loop de loop
All on a Saturday night
You put your right hand in
You take your right hand out
You give your hand a shake, shake, shake
And turn yourself about
Here we go loop de loop
Here we go loop de lie
Here we go loop de loop
All on a Saturday night
You put your left foot in
You take your left foot out
You give your foot a shake, shake, shake
And turn yourself about
Here we go loop de loop
Here we go loop de lie
Here we go loop de loop
All on a Saturday night
You put your right hip in
You take your right hip out
You give your hip a shake, shake, shake
And turn yourself about
Here we go loop de loop
Here we go loop de lie

Here we go loop de loop
All on a Saturday night
You put your whole self in
You take your whole self out
You give yourself a shake, shake, shake
And turn yourself about

Hop a Little, Jump a Little

Hop a little, jump a little,
One, two, three;
Run a little, skip a little,
Tap one knee;
Bend a little, stretch a little,
Nod your head;
Yawn a little, sleep a little,
In your bed.

How Much Wood Would a Woodchuck Chuck

How much wood
would a woodchuck chuck,
if a woodchuck
could chuck wood?
As much wood
As a woodchuck would,
if a woodchuck
could chuck wood.

I Must Not Throw

I must not throw upon the floor
The crust I cannot eat,
For many a hungry little one
Would think it quite a treat.
'Tis wilful waste brings woeful want,
And I may live to say,
Oh, how I wish I had the crust
That once I threw away!

Jesus Loves Me

Jesus loves me! This I know,
For the Bible tells me so.

Little ones to Him belong
They are weak but He is strong.
Yes, Jesus loves me!
Yes, Jesus loves me!
Yes, Jesus loves me!
The Bible tells me so.
Jesus loves me! He who died
Heaven's gate to open wide.
He will wash away my sin
Let His little child come in.
Yes, Jesus loves me!
Yes, Jesus loves me!
Yes, Jesus loves me!
The Bible tells me so.
Jesus loves me! He will stay
Close beside me all the way.
He's prepared a home for me
And some day His face I'll see.
Yes, Jesus loves me!
Yes, Jesus loves me!
Yes, Jesus loves me!
The Bible tells me so.

Once I Caught a Fish Alive

One, two, three, four, five,
Once I caught a fish alive.
Six, seven, eight, nine, ten,
Then I let it go again.
Why did you let it go?
Because it bit my finger so.
Which finger did it bite?
This little finger on the right.

Round and Round the Garden

Round and round the garden
Like a teddy bear,
One step, two step,
Tickle him under there.

Sing Sing

Sing sing, what shall I sing?
The cat has eaten the pudding-string!
Do, do, what shall I do?
The cat has bitten it quite in two.

The Boy in the Barn

A little boy went into the barn,
And lay down on some hay.
An owl came out
And flew about,
And the little boy ran away.

Two Little Hands Go Clap, Clap, Clap

Two little hands go clap, clap, clap.
Two little feet go tap, tap, tap.
Two little eyes are open wide.
One little head goes side to side.

32 Six Lullabies to Soothe Your Baby's Soul

In a world where recorded music is only the push of a button away, we can lose touch with the time-honored tradition of singing to our babies. Singing has long been a method of soothing fussy babies and can be a wonderful way to connect with your baby in an otherwise disjointed day. While you may know the first verse to some of these soothing songs, here's some help with the others.

All Through the Night

Sleep my child and peace attend thee,
All through the night;

Guardian angels God will send thee,
All through the night;
Soft the drowsy hours are creeping,
Hill and vale in slumber sleeping,
I my loved ones' watch am keeping,
All through the night.
Angels watching, e'er around thee,
All through the night;
Midnight slumber close surround thee,
All through the night;
Soft the drowsy hours are creeping,
Hill and vale in slumber sleeping,
I my loved ones' watch am keeping,
All through the night.
While the moon her watch is keeping,
All through the night;
While the weary world is sleeping,
All through the night;
O'er thy spirit gently stealing,
Visions of delight revealing,
Breathes a pure and holy feeling,
All through the night.

Sir Harold Boulton

Angels Watching over Me

All night, all day, angels watching over me, my Lord.
All night, all day, angels watching over me.
Sun is a-setting in the West; angels watching over me,
    my Lord.
Sleep my child, take your rest; angels watching over
    me.
All night, all day, angels watching over me, my Lord.
All night, all day, angels watching over me.

Brahms Lullaby

Lullaby, and good night, with pink roses bedight,
With lilies o'er spread, is my baby's sweet head.

Lay thee down now, and rest, may thy slumber be
  blessed!
Lay thee down now, and rest, may thy slumber be
  blessed!
Lullaby, and good night, your mother's delight,
Shining angels beside my darling abide.
Soft and warm is your bed; close your eyes and rest
  your head.
Soft and warm is your bed; close your eyes and rest
  your head.
Sleepyhead, close your eyes. Mother's right here be-
  side you.
I'll protect you from harm, you will wake in my arms.
Guardian angels are near, so sleep on, with no fear.
Guardian angels are near, so sleep on, with no fear.

Johannes Brahms

Day Is Done

Day is done,
Gone the sun,
From the lake, from the hills, from the sky.
All is well, safely rest,
God is nigh.

Hush Little Baby

Hush, little baby, don't say a word.
Papa's gonna buy you a mockingbird.
And if that mockingbird won't sing,
Papa's gonna buy you a diamond ring.
And if that diamond ring turns brass,
Papa's gonna buy you a looking glass.
And if that looking glass gets broke,
Papa's gonna buy you a billy goat.
And if that billy goat won't pull,
Papa's gonna buy you a cart and bull.
And if that cart and bull turn over,
Papa's gonna buy you a dog named Rover.
And if that dog named Rover won't bark,

Papa's gonna buy you a horse and cart.
And if that horse and cart fall down,
You'll still be the sweetest little baby in town.

Twinkle, Twinkle, Little Star

Twinkle, twinkle, little star
How I wonder what you are,
Up above the world so high,
Like a diamond in the sky.
Twinkle, twinkle, little star
How I wonder what you are!
When the blazing sun is gone,
When he nothing shines upon,
Then you show your little light,
Twinkle, twinkle, all the night.
Twinkle, twinkle, little star,
How I wonder what you are!
Then the traveler in the dark
Thanks you for your tiny spark;
He could not see which way to go,
If you did not twinkle so.
Twinkle, twinkle, little star,
How I wonder what you are!

Jane Taylor

33 Twenty-five Prayers for Your Child

One of the greatest privileges of Christian parenting is praying with your child. Set aside a few minutes each day to talk with God about your baby. As your baby grows, include him in your prayer time. This is a wonderful opportunity to influence your baby's relationship with God as you teach him to engage God in daily conversation.

Pray that:

1. your child will come to know and love God
2. your child and his friends will have salvation
3. your child will have a meaningful relationship with Jesus
4. your child will love others
5. your child will show God's love to others
6. your child will testify to God's goodness in his life
7. godly people will be put in your child's path
8. your child will be a godly person put in the paths of others
9. your child will serve God
10. your child will be obedient to God
11. your child will be obedient to you
12. God will provide for your child's needs
13. your child will trust God
14. your child will give financially to the kingdom of God
15. your child will develop Christlike character
16. your child will have good health, growth, and development
17. your child will have the peace of God
18. your child will have the wisdom of God
19. your child will marry a follower of Christ
20. your child will remain pure until married
21. your child will be in active fellowship with other believers
22. your child will have a healthy and strong church family
23. God will be the source of your child's strength
24. your child will have God's protection
25. your child will stand up for truth

A Prayer Journal

Consider keeping a prayer journal for your child. Write down the prayers that you've prayed for your child and record God's faithfulness in answering your prayers. Your child will be able to read and reflect on this journal in years to come.

Traditional Irish Baby Blessing

May all the blessing of our Lord touch your life today.
May He send His little angels to protect you on your way.
Such a wee little fit, sent from above,
Someone so precious to cherish and love.
May sunshine and moonbeams dance over your head,
As you quietly slumber in your bed.
May good luck be with you wherever you go.
And your blessings outnumber the shamrocks that grow.

34 Recommended Resources for Parents of Babies

At one time or another, every parent needs some help. Whether it is practical advice for a parenting dilemma or the current recommendations on vaccinations, we all need some place to turn for quality information and guidance.

Local Resources

Your pediatrician's office, local library, community center, play space, coffee shop bulletin board, hospital, town recreation department, and churches are great places to locate information on parenting resources in your area.

Books

These books are a great addition to any new parent's library.

Title	Author	Topic
American Academy of Pediatrics Baby and Child Health	American Academy of Pediatrics	health
Caring for Your Baby and Young Child: Birth to Age 5, revised edition	American Academy of Pediatrics	general
Everything You Need to Know about Your Baby: Birth to Age Two	William Sears, Martha Sears, Robert Sears, and James Sears	general
Experts' Guide to the Baby Years: 100 Things Every Parent Should Know	Samantha Ettus	general
Grace Based Parenting	Tim Kimmel	parenting
Nanny to the Rescue!	Michelle LaRowe	parenting
Ready or Not Here We Come! The Real Experts' Guide to the First Year with Twins	Elizabeth Lyons	parenting twins
Single Parenting That Works	Dr. Kevin Leman	single parenting
Solve Your Child's Sleep Problems	Richard Ferber, MD	sleep
Super Baby Food	Ruth Yaron	food
What to Expect the First Year	Heidi Murkoff, Sandy Hathaway, Arlene Eisenberg	general
The Womanly Art of Breastfeeding	La Leche League International	breastfeeding
Working Mom's 411	Michelle LaRowe	working mothers

133

Organizations

These organizations provide a wealth of important information for parents of babies.

Organization	Website	Resource for
American Academy of Pediatrics	http://www.aap.org/	children's health and development
American Association of Poison Control Centers	http://www.aapcc.org/DNN/	poison control
American SIDS Institute	http://www.sids.org/index.htm	SIDS prevention
Centers for Disease Control and Prevention	http://www.cdc.gov/	health information
Consumer Product Safety Commission	http://www.cpsc.gov/	safety alerts and recalls
Focus on the Family	http://www.focusonthefamily.com/	Christian parenting
International Nanny Association	http://www.nanny.org/	nanny care
La Leche League International	http://www.llli.org/	breastfeeding
Safe Kids USA	http://www.usa.safekids.org/	prevention of accidental injuries
Women, Infants and Children (WIC)	http://www.fns.usda.gov/wic/	low income families

LISTS FOR THE TODDLER YEARS

35 Nutritional Guidelines for Toddlers

The American Academy of Pediatrics recommends that children from ages 1 to 3 should eat 40 calories per inch of height each day. This means that the average toddler needs 1,000 to 1,400 calories per day.

To be sure that your toddler gets the recommended daily amounts of vitamins and minerals needed for healthy growth, it's important that you offer your toddler a variety of foods daily.

The USDA recommends that per day, toddlers eat:

6 servings of grain

3 servings of vegetables

2 servings of fruit

2 servings of meat

2 servings of milk (Toddlers may eat 4½ servings from the milk group each day.) [1]

Sample Serving Sizes for Toddlers

1 grain serving	½ slice of bread; ¼ cup cooked rice, cereal, or pasta; ½ pancake; ½ bun, roll, or tortilla; or ½ cup cereal
1 vegetable serving	¼ to ½ cup cooked veggies or ½ cup 100 percent vegetable juice
1 fruit serving	¼ to ½ cup fruit or ½ cup 100 percent fruit juice
1 meat serving	1 ounce cooked meat, poultry, or fish; 1 cooked egg; or ¼ cup dry beans
1 milk serving	1 cup yogurt; 1 cup whole milk; or 2 ounces of cheese

Tips for Feeding Your Toddler

Always be sure that your toddler is seated when eating.

Use kitchen shears to cut bite-sized pieces of your toddler's food.

Cut hot dogs lengthwise twice before slicing across and feeding to your toddler. Tough skin should be removed. Round shaped pieces are a choking hazard.

Encourage your toddler to try everything. Some toddlers will have to be introduced to a food several times before they acquire a taste for it.

Food Choking Hazards for Toddlers

dried fruit

gum

hard candy

hot dogs (cut in round pieces)

ice cubes

marshmallows

popcorn

potato chips

pretzels

raisins

raw carrots and celery

36 How Much Sleep Do Toddlers Need?

Richard Ferber, MD, director of the Center for Pediatric Sleep Disorders at Children's Hospital in Boston and author of

Solve Your Child's Sleep Problems, recommends that toddlers sleep between 11 and 12 hours per 24-hour period. Although some toddlers may sleep more and some may sleep less, the following chart shows how a typical toddler sleeps.

Typical Toddler Sleep Requirements[2]

Age	Total Sleep (hours)	Nighttime Sleep (hours)	Daytime Sleep (hours)
1 year	11¾	9¾	2
2 years	11½	[10]	1½
3 years	11¼	10¼	1

Transitioning from Two Naps to One

By 18 months of age, most toddlers are ready to transition from two naps to one. A midafternoon nap, starting between 1 and 2 p.m., can help avoid a major meltdown before dinner.

From Crib to Bed

When your toddler reaches 35 inches or can climb over the side of her crib, it is time to transition her to a bed. Toddler beds that sit close to the floor and have a safety rail are a great option.

37 The Best Bedtime Routine

During the toddler years, it is important to help your child develop good sleep habits. Having a solid bedtime routine helps ensure that your toddler gets an adequate amount of sleep each night and helps to foster good sleep habits that will continue through adulthood.

Consider these tips when establishing your toddler's bedtime routine.

- *Have a set time for dinner.* Most families of toddlers find that eating dinner between 4:30 and 5:30 works best. Eating later than 5:30 tends to push a toddler's bedtime back too late.
- *Begin winding down your toddler's day after mealtime.* After dinner encourage your child to play board games, read, or do other activities that won't get him wound up.
- *Have a set time for bed.* A toddler should be in bed between 7:00 and 7:30 p.m. Give your child notice when bedtime is approaching.
- *Make bath time part of your bedtime routine.* A warm bath can help a child relax and can signal his body that bedtime is approaching.
- *Avoid foods that tend to energize your child before bed.* Chocolate and sugary snacks are popular culprits. Drinks are also a no-no an hour before lights out.
- *Allow your child to read a book or watch a short age-appropriate video as part of his bedtime routine.* Bedtime stories or animated books on DVD are good choices.
- *Have your child pick out his own pajamas.* Allowing your child to have a say in what he sleeps in gives him a feeling that he shares control over his bedtime routine. Allowing your toddler to feel that he has some control can help avoid other bedtime battles.
- *Make good night, good night.* Avoid prolonged farewells and returning to your child's room for just one more kiss or hug. This only prolongs the inevitable and gives your child a false sense of hope that bedtime can be bumped back.

Recommended Bedtime Routine for Toddlers

4:30–5:30 p.m. dinner

5:30–6:00 p.m. quiet play

6:00–6:30 p.m. bath

6:30–7:00 p.m. bedtime story or video

7:00–7:30 p.m. lights out

38 Stature and Weight Guidelines for Toddlers

The term *toddler* is generally used to define children from 18 months to 3 years of age. You can expect your toddler to grow, on average, about half a pound per month.[3] By 2 years of age, your toddler may weigh four times her birth weight and may measure in at about 34 inches.[4] Between the ages of 2 and 3, your toddler may gain on average 3–5 pounds and 3 inches.[5]

The Picky Eater

During the toddler years, you may have your first encounter with a picky eater. It can take a child eight or more interactions with a new food before she'll truly try it, so if your child passes on her peas the first time around, don't give up. Continue to introduce them to her. You may also want to take advantage of a cookbook with recipes that "hide" nutrition in foods your child already likes. *The Sneaky Chef* and *Deceptively Delicious* are two such cookbooks that you may want to check out!

2 to 20 years: Boys
Stature-for-age and Weight-for-age percentiles

NAME _____

RECORD # _____

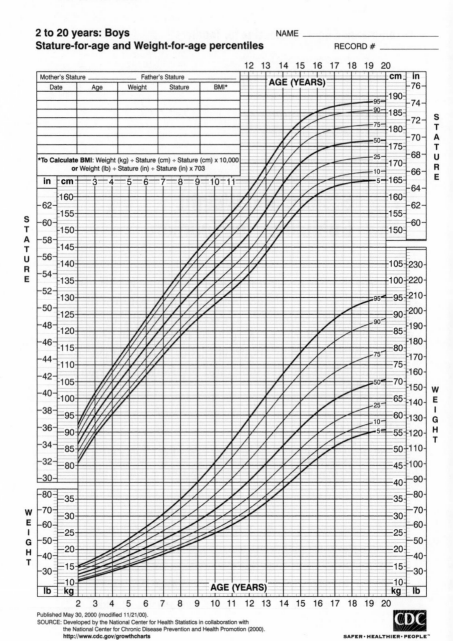

Published May 30, 2000 (modified 11/21/00).
SOURCE: Developed by the National Center for Health Statistics in collaboration with
the National Center for Chronic Disease Prevention and Health Promotion (2000).
http://www.cdc.gov/growthcharts

CDC
SAFER·HEALTHIER·PEOPLE™

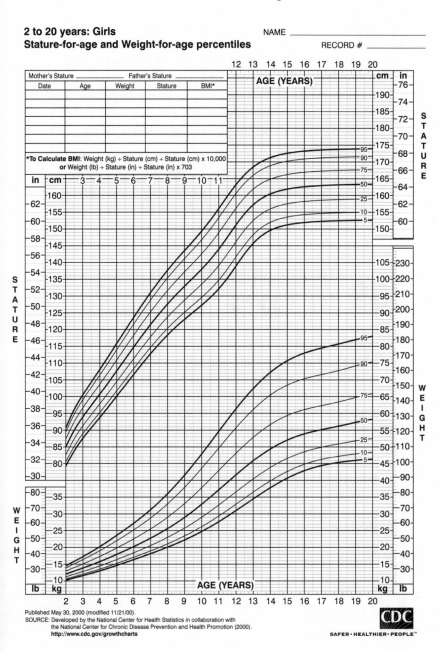

2 to 20 years: Girls
Stature-for-age and Weight-for-age percentiles

NAME _____

RECORD # _____

Published May 30, 2000 (modified 11/21/00).
SOURCE: Developed by the National Center for Health Statistics in collaboration with
the National Center for Chronic Disease Prevention and Health Promotion (2000).
http://www.cdc.gov/growthcharts

SAFER·HEALTHIER·PEOPLE™

143

Grazing

You may notice that your toddler prefers to graze over the course of the day, rather than sit and eat full meals. Have healthy choices like fresh fruits and vegetables available to serve your toddler throughout the day. Use an ice cube tray filled with bite-sized nutritious and colorful options, such as small pieces of cheese, an assortment of colorful fruits and vegetables, and soft whole-wheat crackers. These snacks can ensure that your toddler gets a well-balanced selection that interests her.

39 Developmental Milestones for Toddlers

Every toddler will develop intellectually, socially, and physically at his own pace, but there are some milestones that most children reach during the ages of 12 to 36 months. The following is a standard checklist of developmental benchmarks you can expect your 1 to 3 year old to reach. Most parenting resources will list a variation of these widely accepted milestones to help you assess your toddler's growth and development.

By the End of 18 Months

Physical

Most children can:

✓ crawl well
✓ stand alone

✓ sit alone
✓ pull off hats or socks
✓ turn pages in a book
✓ stack two blocks
✓ poke, twist, and squeeze things
✓ pull, push, and dump things
✓ close doors
✓ carry around small objects
✓ hold a spoon
✓ walk without assistance
✓ wave bye-bye
✓ hold a crayon

Intellectual

Most children can:

✓ recognize themselves in a mirror and in pictures
✓ identify objects in books
✓ point at what they want
✓ understand and follow one-step instructions
✓ play peekaboo

Social and Emotional

Most children can:

✓ say eight to twenty words
✓ use expressions like "uh-oh" or "oops"
✓ look at people when they are talking to them
✓ experience separation anxiety
✓ imitate others
✓ soak up the applause from an audience

By the End of 24 Months

Physical

Most children can:

- ✓ walk well
- ✓ run
- ✓ feed themselves with a toddler-sized spoon
- ✓ stack two to four blocks
- ✓ toss a ball
- ✓ open cabinets and drawers
- ✓ pick up toys without falling over
- ✓ walk up steps with assistance
- ✓ begin to gain bowel and bladder control

Intellectual

Most children can:

- ✓ exert independence by saying no
- ✓ sit through short stories
- ✓ begin to show preferences for toys and people
- ✓ point to parts of the body
- ✓ respond to prompting
- ✓ talk to self-express

Social and Emotional

Most children can:

- ✓ say hundreds of words
- ✓ use two-to-three-word sentences
- ✓ repeat words that they hear
- ✓ sing

✓ resist sharing
✓ have a hard time waiting
✓ have temper tantrums
✓ use the words *me* and *mine*
✓ enjoy attention
✓ hit or bite when frustrated
✓ show affection
✓ get frustrated
✓ become attached to a favorite blanket or toy

By the End of 36 Months

Physical

Most children can:

✓ ride a tricycle
✓ climb
✓ run and jump in place
✓ draw a straight line
✓ wash and dry hands
✓ stand on one foot for a moment
✓ walk up stairs
✓ build a tower six to eight blocks high
✓ open doors by turning a knob
✓ pull a wagon
✓ string beads
✓ snip with scissors
✓ turn single paper pages of a book
✓ work latches
✓ put some of their clothes on
✓ untie shoes

✓ use the potty

Intellectual

Most children can:

✓ need time to transition to activities
✓ sort colors
✓ identify at least one color
✓ draw a face
✓ make associations
✓ understand the concepts 1 and 2
✓ count a few objects
✓ solve simple problems
✓ follow three-step instructions

Social and Emotional

Most children can:

✓ speak in sentences of five to six words in length
✓ speak clearly enough for nonfamily members to understand
✓ ask questions
✓ tell stories
✓ use color and sizes to identify objects
✓ show a sense of ownership
✓ wait their turn
✓ ask for help when needed
✓ display independence

Building Boundaries

Toddlers begin to develop a sense of independence and test the limits of people and things around them. Now is the time to build nonnegotiable boundaries when it comes to safety, house rules, and behavior.

Six Tools to Tame Your Toddler's Behavior

1. redirection
2. distraction
3. diversion
4. setting limits
5 structure
6. time-outs

40 The Toddler's Toy Box

The general rule of thumb when choosing toys for your toddler is less is more. The more bells and whistles a toy has, the less there is for your toddler to do. Simple toys that promote exploration, independence, problem solving, and pretending will engage your child best during this stage of development. Animals and dolls to nurture and cuddle, props to mimic activities that you do around the house, and toys that promote muscle development, hand-eye coordination, and small and large motor skills are developmentally appropriate choices.

Toys for Your 12 to 24 Month Old

balls, various types and sizes
egg shakers
large Lego toys
lock-and-key toys

nesting toys
peekaboo books
peg or knob puzzles with three to five pieces
pop-up toys
pounding toys
push-and-pull toys
shape sorters
simple train
stacking cups
straddle-ride toys
stuffed toys
toy phone
toys and containers for dumping and sorting
tunnels for crawling through
wooden blocks

Toys for Your 2 to 3 Year Old

cars
doll carriage
doll house
dolls
dough and clay
dress up clothing
games of matching
large beads and string for lacing
large blocks
large cardboard bricks
large pieces of paper, crayons, and paint
peg boards
plastic tools

a play kitchen and accessories
props for pretend play
puppets
realistic looking ride-on toys
small plastic climbing structures and slides
tricycles
trucks
water and sand tables
wooden puzzles

Toddler Tip

Toddlers can handle only a limited selection of toy choices while they play. Encourage your toddler to play with only a few toys at a time or rotate your child's toys each week so she has the opportunity to explore everything.

41 The Toddler's Library

Little hands need little books, and books that are sturdy and resistant to chewing and drooling make cloth and board books the perfect choice for your toddler. Books with repetition, rhyming words, and great illustrations will capture your toddler's attention. As your toddler grows, lift-the-flap books and pop-up books will become fun favorites. Toddlers seem to love animal books especially and often begin talking by repeating the sounds that a cow, dog, or rooster makes. So cute!

Thirty-five Books You and Your Toddler Will Love

1. *Goodnight Moon* by Margaret Wise Brown
2. *Big Red Barn* by Margaret Wise Brown
3. *The Runaway Bunny* by Margaret Wise Brown
4. *I See* by Rachel Isadora
5. *Pat the Bunny* by Dorothy Kunhardt
6. *Dr. Seuss's ABC: An Amazing Alphabet Book!* by Dr. Seuss
7. *Mr. Brown Can Moo, Can You?* by Dr. Seuss
8. *Happy Baby: Colors* by Rodger Priddy
9. *Olivia* by Ian Falconer
10. *Brown Bear, Brown Bear What Do You See?* by Bill Martin Jr.
11. *Where's Spot?* by Eric Hill
12. *The Very Busy Spider* by Eric Carle
13. *The Very Hungry Caterpillar* by Eric Carle
14. *Peek-a-Boo* by Molly Bang
15. *Bless This Day: Toddler Prayers* by Anne E. Kitch and Joni Oeltjenbruns
16. *Max's Breakfast* by Rosemary Wells
17. *Moo, Baa, La La La* by Sandra Boynton
18. *The Going to Bed Book* by Sandra Boynton
19. *Dinosaur's Binkit* by Sandra Boynton
20. *Teeth Are Not for Biting* by Elizabeth Verdick and Marieka Heinlen
21. *Teddy in the House* by Lucy Cousins
22. *Noah's Ark* by Lucy Cousins
23. *I Spy Little Book* by Jean Marzollo
24. *Things That Go* by Amanda Barlow
25. *Things That Move* by Jo Litchfield
26. *My Favorite Bible Stories for Toddlers* by Dalmatian Press
27. *Lift the Flap Bible* by Reader's Digest Children
28. *Wheels on the Bus* by DK Publishing

29. *My Quiet Book, Soft Activity Book* by Pockets of Learning
30. *My First Word Book* by Angela Wilkes
31. *Guess How Much I Love You* by Sam McBratney
32. *Goodnight Gorilla* by Peggy Rathmann
33. *Baby Beluga* by Raffi
34. *Chicka Chicka ABC* by John Archambault and Bill Martin Jr.
35. *Jamberry* by Bruce Degan

Tips for Reading to Your Toddler

- *Choose books with pictures and illustrations that show kids doing things they do every day.* Books with pictures of babies eating, bathing, clapping, and going to bed are great choices.
- *Choose books about topics that interest your toddler.* If your toddler loves trucks, read truck books. If he loves animals, read books about animals.
- *Don't be surprised if your toddler asks to read the same book over and over again.* Toddlers love repetition because the predictable pattern empowers them as they learn to know what to expect.
- *Get creative and use different voices for different characters.* Your toddler will love you for it!
- *Point to the items in the illustrations and name them.* Labeling is a wonderful way to teach your child that things have names and what those names are.
- *Keep books in an easy-to-access place to encourage your toddler to explore them on his own.* A basket on the floor is a great place for your toddler's books.
- *Visit your library and let your toddler pick out books to bring home.*

- *Set aside time each day to read to your toddler.* Reading can help him develop his vocabulary, learn letter identification, and understand that writing on the pages represents words.
- *You'll know that your toddler is ready to transition to paper-paged books* when he begins to turn the pages on his own and no longer puts books in his mouth.

Story Time

Most local libraries host no-cost toddler story times. Take advantage of these read-aloud opportunities. Your child will benefit from listening to others read, and you may pick up some read-aloud pointers.

42 Twenty Terrific Activities Toddlers Love

Toddlers learn by doing. Engaging your toddler in activities that allow her to learn about her environment, explore new things, and exert her independence will be enjoyed. Also toddlers want to be grown-up, so don't be surprised if your child enjoys helping you clean the house or make dinner or care for a younger sibling.

Twenty Toddler-Tested Activities

1. pudding painting
2. sponge painting
3. empty soda bottle bowling
4. bubble blowing
5. stringing large pasta on yarn

6. playing with dough
7. hiding and seeking objects
8. collecting leaves
9. making a house out of an appliance box
10. feeding the ducks
11. playing in a band
12. having a picnic
13. visiting a farm or petting zoo
14. taking a trip to the library
15. making instant pudding
16. playing follow the leader
17. dancing to music
18. playing dress up
19. playing freeze dance
20. straw painting

How to Make Play Dough

Ingredients:

1 cup of water
1 tablespoon vegetable oil
½ cup of salt
1 tablespoon cream of tarter
food coloring
1 cup of flour

Directions:

1. Combine water, oil, salt, cream of tartar, and food coloring in a saucepan.
2. Heat until mixture is warm.
3. Remove pan from heat and add flour.
4. Stir the mixture and then knead until smooth.
5. Store dough in an airtight container or in a freezer bag.

LIST
43 Guilt-Free DVDs for Your Toddler

Whether it is time to take a phone call or to shoot off an email, every parent needs a short break occasionally. These videos give you a guilt-free option for entertaining your toddler during the times when you need a few minutes to yourself.

Baby Signing Time (Two Little Hands Production). This DVD will give you and your toddler an enjoyable and easy introduction to baby sign language. You'll learn basic signs together that will help end the frustrations associated with the preverbal communication barrier.

Booples! 2: Yikitty Blar! (Booples). This Dove Family Approved favorite teaches toddlers Bible verses and introduces them to Scripture memory. The DVD provides a fun way to teach young children Bible basics.

Bop Along with the Bop-a-Lots (Wonderful). Cute characters will introduce your toddler to their classic songs sung to a different beat. "Old MacDonald" is sung in Dixieland style, and "Rock-a-Bye Baby" to a calypso beat.

Brainy Baby Shapes and Colors (Brainy Baby Music). Live action films of children make learning shapes and colors easy and fun. This DVD introduces twelve shapes and colors and has special features, including a video sing-along and other interactive activities.

Chicka Chicka Boom Boom and Lots More Learning Fun (Scholastic Video Collection). The classic children's book hits the little screen as the letters of the alphabet dance their way up the coconut tree. A great reinforcement to your daily read-aloud time.

Classical Baby 3-Pack (HBO). Masterpieces of fine art, music, and dance are brought to life in *Classical Baby Art*, *Classical Baby Dance*, and *Classical Baby Music*. Educational and engaging, your toddler will stop what he's doing and take note. This DVD was a 2007 National Parent Publications Award winner.

Harold and the Purple Crayon: Let Your Imagination Soar (Sony Pictures). Based on the classic book, Harold will help toddlers unlock their imagination. Full of entertaining episodes, Harold teaches children about forgiveness and friendship.

Little Noah (Little Learners). The Bible story of Noah is told in this creative DVD, which is complete with Bible songs sung by the Little Learners choir. As toddlers watch this video, they can listen to it in their choice of languages.

My Learning Steps: Learning My ABCs (My Learning Steps). Parents have the option to personalize this video and narrate it themselves! It teaches children their ABCs through colorful, playful, and engaging songs and animation. This video received five out of five Doves for family viewing by the Dove Foundation.

Once Upon a Potty for Girls/Once Upon a Potty for Boys (Barron's Educational Studios). The popular children's books by Alona Frankel are now animated programs. Viewers can follow Prudence or Joshua's lead as they transition from diapers to the potty. The DVD also features the silly and beloved "Potty Song."

The Dove Foundation

Since 1991 the Dove Foundation has been encouraging and promoting quality, family-friendly entertainment that is based on Judeo/Christian values. Visit their website at www.dove.org to learn more about a movie before you rent or buy it. You can also look for the "Family-Approved" seal on Dove approved videos.

TV Time for Toddlers

Once your child hits age 2, limit your toddler's viewing time to no more than 1 hour per day. The American Academy of Pediatrics recommends that children under age 2 watch no television at all.

44 Twenty Musical Moments for Toddlers

Music is more than entertainment for your toddler; it can foster social, emotional, and cognitive development. Not only does exposing your toddler to different types of music and sounds evoke strong emotions and encourage communication, it can help form additional pathways between the cells in her brain. These connections or pathways will help your child later in school, especially with learning languages and math.

During the toddler years, provide your child with daily opportunities to experience actively various types of music. Here are twenty ways:

1. Sing songs that have hand motions or encourage movement, like "The Wheels on the Bus" or "The Hokey Pokey."
2. Sing songs that are finger plays, like "Five Little Ducklings."

3. Encourage your toddler to clap, sway, or march to music.

4. Make up silly songs and sing them to your child.

5. Personalize song lyrics by adding your child's name.

6. Purchase instruments for your toddler to play, such as bells, egg shakers, rattles, and tambourines.

7. Introduce props like scarves, hats, and stuffed animals for your toddler to use while dancing.

8. Dance with your toddler.

9. Play musical games with your child. Clap out a rhythm and encourage your child to clap it back.

10. Give your child a pot and wooden spoon to bang on while you're cooking dinner.

11. Enroll your toddler in a quality mommy-and-me music program, like Music Together.

12. Expose your toddler to various types of music by playing classical, folk, and other styles.

13. Sing new lyrics to familiar tunes. Encourage your child to make up a verse to his favorite song.

14. Tap out the beat with your foot while chanting or singing nursery rhymes.

15. Sing songs to coach your kids through cleanup time and bath time.

16. Play soft, gentle music as a signal to your child that it's bedtime.

17. Turn on the music while your toddler finger paints or colors.

18. Have a family marching band. Everyone can grab an instrument and march around the house.

19. Sing a conversation, rather than speaking it.

20. Teach your child to hum a tune.

Toddler Music That Kids *and* Moms Love

Music Together Song Collections, available at www.musictogether .com

On a Flying Guitar by Steve Songs, available at www.stevesongs
.com

A–Z Alphabet Animal Songs by David Polansky, available at www
.davidpolansky.com

Jesus Loves You Personalized Christian Music by Kid Music, available at www.kidmusic.com

Maestro Classics Stories in Music Series, available at www.magic
maestromusic.com

45 Ten Life Lessons to Teach Your Toddler

There are some life lessons that every child should learn, and
there is no better time to teach children than during the toddler years. The toddler years provide a unique opportunity
to begin teaching your child important life lessons, because
by nature, toddlers are curious, eager to please, and ready to
imitate. Take advantage of this time and start teaching your
toddler these ten important lessons for life.

1. *Jesus loves you—and the kids that you don't like.* Often
   we teach the first part of this lesson and forego the
   second. Teach your child to recognize that God loves
   everybody, equally and always.
2. *Everyone is different.* Everyone is uniquely made. Teach
   your child that different doesn't always mean good or
   bad.
3. No *means no.* Instill a clear understanding of no in
   your toddler. Children aren't born ready to respect;
   they learn over time as they test your boundaries.
4. *How to share.* While your child is young, encourage a
   spirit of generosity. Teach your child to take turns and

to share his toys with others. This lesson also lays the foundation for teaching the importance of cooperation and teamwork.

5. *Patience.* This isn't something that comes naturally, and for most, patience is a hard lesson to learn. Waiting in line, waiting at a restaurant for a meal, and waiting to get a new toy are opportunities to practice patience with your child.

6. *Good hygiene.* Your child's future spouse will be very thankful if you instill this lesson in your child. Teach your child to bathe daily, brush his teeth regularly, and wash his hands often.

7. *Manners.* Practicing good manners doesn't have to be a lost art. Model good manners for your child. From saying please and thank you to holding the door open for others, manners can make a comeback!

8. *Hard work.* Giving it your all is important. Teach your child to complete what he starts and not give up. You'll teach your child that he can do anything.

9. *How to be healthy.* From eating nutritiously to exercising daily, teach your children the importance of living a healthy lifestyle and taking care of their bodies.

10. *You can't identify a "bad person" by the way he or she looks.* Often parents make the mistake of teaching their children that strangers or dangerous people look a certain way. The truth is they don't. It's important to let your kids know that there's no way to tell if a person is bad just by looking at him or her.

Three Effective Ways to Teach Your Toddler

1. Set the example.
2. Role play.
3. Take advantage of natural learning moments.

46 Five Great Everyday Ways to Teach Your Toddler about God

By capitalizing on natural learning moments throughout the day, you can teach your toddler about God and his great love for us and others. Look for opportunities to communicate things to your child about our Father, Creator, and Friend.

1. *Point out God's creations.* Take the opportunity to point out to your toddler all of the wonderful things God has created. Introduce basic Bible lessons, such as, "The birds don't have to worry about what they will eat or wear because God takes care of them and he will take care of us too."
2. *Praise God.* Show your child that you recognize God's goodness, provisions, and blessings by thanking him regularly for what he is doing in the life of your family. Remember to praise God in the bad times as well, and allow your toddler to see you ask God for help in times of trouble.
3. *Pray together.* Talk to God together before meals and before bed. Let your child see and hear you pray daily and encourage your child to chime in. Let your toddler know when God answers your prayers.
4. *Choose media that communicate Bible truths.* Bible songs on CD and movies and shows that communicate basic Bible truths provide a fun way for your child to learn about God. She may even share what she knows with others.
5. *Foster a servant's heart in your child.* Provide opportunities for your toddler to serve others. Even the littlest

of hands can sprinkle jimmies on cookies or make a
picture to give to a sick or elderly friend.

Celebrate the Birth of Christ

It can be easy to get caught up in the Christmas season
and forget to teach our children the reason Christians
celebrate Christmas. Throw a birthday party for Jesus,
complete with a cake to celebrate the birth of Christ.
Purchasing gifts and giving them to needy families
in honor of Jesus's birthday is a great and practical
way to demonstrate to your toddler the love Christ has
for others.

47 Easy Steps for Taming Your Toddler's Tantrums

Although the frequency and intensity may vary, all toddlers, at
one time or another, have tantrums. Tantrums are a powerful
way for a toddler to communicate his frustrations. Because toddlers don't yet have the language or the self-control to express
their feelings in more acceptable ways, they resort to communi-
cating in a powerful way that will surely grab your attention.

To tame your toddler's tantrum:

1. *Stay calm.* You can't expect your child to regain control
   if you lose yours.
2. *Ignore the tantrum.* If your toddler is in a safe place,
   continue on with what you were doing without giving
   any attention to your child's outburst.
3. *Give a warning if the tantrum doesn't stop.* If ignoring
   your child doesn't work, give him a specific warning

with a specific, immediate consequence: "I'm going to count to three, and if you don't stop screaming, we are going to leave the store [or you'll get a time-out or you'll lose the privilege of playing with that toy]."

4. *Follow through with the consequences.* This is one instance when you'll have to mean what you say and say what you mean. Lack of follow-through is the strongest indicator of whether future warnings will work.

5. *Wait for your child to cool down and then validate feelings without validating behavior.* Once your toddler has calmed down, let him know that you understand he was mad (frustrated, tired, or sad), but when we are mad, we don't scream (or hit or roll on the floor).

6. *Give alternative suggestions on handling feelings.* Give your toddler words that will communicate how he is feeling. Say something like: "When we are mad, we say, 'I'm mad.'"

Tips to Prevent a Toddler Tantrum

- *Be clear with your expectations and explanations.* Give short and simple instructions and resist the urge to negotiate or give long-winded lectures.

- *Be consistent with your rules, consequences, and follow-through.* Consistency will determine how often and how bad your toddler's tantrums will be.

- *Be careful not to set your toddler up for a tantrum.* Taking a tired or hungry kid out and about is a tantrum waiting to happen.

- *Don't give in to a tantrum.* If you do, the next one is going to be like the song says: a little bit louder and a whole lot worse.

⫿⫿S⫿ Ten Recommended Reads
48 for Parents of Toddlers

With all the books out there, it can be hard to know which books share your parenting philosophy and offer solid and practical parenting advice. These ten books are a great addition to any parent's library.

1. *1-2-3 Magic for Christian Parents: Effective Discipline for Children 2–12* by Thomas Phelan
2. *The Complete Book of Christian Parenting and Childcare* by Dr. William and Martha Sears
3. *The Five Love Languages of Children* by Gary Chapman and Ross Campbell
4. *Nanny to the Rescue!* by Michelle LaRowe
5. *The New Dare to Discipline* by Dr. James Dobson
6. *The New Strong-Willed Child* by Dr. James Dobson
7. *Parenting the Way God Parents: Refusing to Recycle Your Parents' Mistakes* by Katherine Koonce
8. *The Power of a Praying Parent* by Stormie Ormartian
9. *Toddler Café: Fast, Healthy, and Fun Ways to Feed Even the Pickiest Eater* by Jennifer and Matthew Carden
10. *What to Expect the Toddler Years* by Arlene Eisenberg, Heidi Murkoff, and Sandee Hathaway

Does Your Favorite Parenting Book Present a Biblical View of Discipline?

When reading parenting books or getting parenting advice about discipline, be sure it lines up with biblical truths. Here's an outline of what biblical discipline is.

1. ***Discipline is discipling.*** Literally discipline means "to teach and to raise up." In fact, it comes from the same word as disciple. When Peter talked about being a disciple, he described "men who have been with us the whole time the Lord Jesus went in and out among us, beginning with John's baptism to the time when Jesus was taken up from us" (Acts 1:21–22).

2. ***Discipline is an act of love.*** "I have loved you with an everlasting love," God told his people in Jeremiah 31:3 at a time in their history when he was also judging their sin. The intent of discipline is to guide and direct a child on the right path. The goal of discipline is to teach children to live in a way that is honoring to God, their parents, and themselves. The parent who disciplines a child is instilling and fine-tuning the child's inner compass, which she will use to navigate through life.

3. ***Discipline is proactive.*** Discipline is a way of life. It requires setting clear limits, boundaries, and expectations for a child, and being consistent in holding a child accountable to them. "Impress [God's commandments] on your children. Talk about them when you sit at home and when you walk along the road, when you lie down and when you get up" (Deut. 6:7). When a child fails to adhere to these established standards, discipline requires an action to be taken. This action could be a heart-to-heart conversation, a time-out, or a loss of a privilege, but the goal of the action is to reinforce that a behavior is unacceptable, not to cause pain or deep hurt to the child.

4. *Discipline is a process.* Discipline is not a "one-time fix" for anything. It's the process of instilling your family values, morals, and beliefs into your child by adjusting your limits, boundaries, and expectations as your child grows. The book of Judges describes Israel's national rebellion against God this way: "After that whole generation had been gathered to their fathers, another generation grew up, who knew neither the Lord nor what he had done for Israel" (2:10). In other words, the process of discipline broke down over the years, and a generation was lost.

5. *Discipline's effects are permanent.* Discipline yields lifelong patterns. "Train a child in the way he should go, and when he is old he will not turn from it" (Prov. 22:6). Simply put, when your child is taught to behave in a certain way and is held to certain standards consistently, these behaviors and standards become her norm, because she doesn't know anything else. (Now, when kids start school and as they become teenagers, there may be a detour or two in their road, but when you train them according to their unique makeup, much like the way a gardener will gently "train" ivy to climb a wall, they'll always find their way back to the right path.)

LISTS FOR THE PRESCHOOL YEARS

49 Sleep Guidelines for Preschoolers

The term *preschooler* is generally used to define children 3 to 5 years of age. Most preschoolers require 10 to 12 hours of sleep per 24-hour period.

How a preschooler's sleep time is broken up can depend on the child. Some children will sleep a solid 12 hours over the course of a night; others may sleep 9 hours but require a 1- to 2-hour afternoon nap.

During the preschool years, many children protest having a nap, but because of their energetic activity level, most 3 to 5 year olds will still benefit from a short nap every day throughout their preschool years. Preschoolers can usually benefit from as little as a 1-hour nap in the midafternoon.

If your child refuses to take a nap, set aside an hour each day for your preschooler to rest and recharge.

The Preschooler's Bedroom

To promote good sleep habits, your preschooler's bedroom must be conducive to sleeping.

To help create an environment that promotes sleep:

Do not allow your child to have a television in his bedroom.

Make the bed for sleeping only.

Keep the bedroom organized and understimulating. Brightly colored wall paint, bold lighting, or other decor that commands your child's attention can distract from sleeping.

Keep the room slightly cool. Most children sleep best in rooms that are 68–69 degrees Fahrenheit.

If you must keep the lights on, choose a small night-light that offers a soft glow, rather than leaving on a bedroom or hallway light.

50 Nutritional Guidelines for Preschoolers

Preschoolers require about 1,200 to 1,600 calories per day.[1] Preschool-age children should get their daily calories from three well-balanced meals and two healthy snacks. The United States Department of Agriculture's (USDA) My Pyramid for Preschoolers website (www.mypyramid.gov/preschoolers) can help you assure that your child eats a variety of foods in age-appropriate portions.

Daily Recommendations by Food Group[2]

Food Group	Children Ages 2–3 Years Old	Children Ages 4–8 Years Old
Grains	3 ounce equivalents	4–5 ounce equivalents
	*In general, 1 slice of bread, 1 cup of ready-to-eat cereal, or ½ cup cooked rice, cooked pasta, or cooked cereal can be considered as 1 ounce equivalent from the grain group.	

Food Group	Children Ages 2–3 Years Old	Children Ages 4–8 Years Old
Vegetables	1 cup	1½ cups
	*In general, 1 cup of raw or cooked vegetables or vegetable juice, or 2 cups of raw leafy greens can be considered as 1 cup from the vegetable group.	
Fruits	1 cup	1 to 1½ cups
	*In general, 1 cup of fruit or 100 percent fruit juice, or ½ cup of dried fruit can be considered as 1 cup from the fruit group.	
Milk	2 cups	2 cups
	*In general 1 cup of milk or yogurt, 1½ ounces of natural cheese, or 2 ounces of processed cheese can be considered as 1 cup from the milk group.	
Meat and Beans	2 ounce equivalents	3–4 ounce equivalents
	*In general, 1 ounce of meat, poultry, or fish, ¼ cup of cooked dry beans, 1 egg, 1 tablespoon of peanut butter, or ½ ounce of nuts or seeds can be considered as 1 ounce equivalent from the meat and bean group.	

More information about food groups, daily allowances, and measurements may be found online at www.mypyramid .gov/pyramid.

Mealtime Tips for Parents of Preschoolers

- *Serve regularly scheduled meals and snacks.* Preschoolers should be weaned out of the grazing phase and should be encouraged to eat on a schedule.

- *Keep mealtime focused on food and family.* Do not allow toys or TV while eating dinner. The dinner table is a great time for the family to reconnect during the day. Children who dine with their parents eat healthier meals and are less likely to engage in risky social behavior.[3]

- *Set the example.* Your preschooler will be looking to mimic how and what you eat. Make healthy choices, and your child will too.

- *Encourage your child to eat a variety of foods* by regularly introducing new choices along with his standard favorites.
- *Don't force a child to eat everything on his plate.* Instead, encourage your child to stop eating when he feels full.

Popular Snacks for Preschoolers

string cheese
single-serving yogurts
dried fruit
fresh fruit
baby carrots
whole grain crackers

Problem Portions

- *Juice.* Limit your preschooler's juice intake to no more than 4 to 6 ounces of 100 percent fruit juice per day.
- *Soda.* Soda provides empty calories that offer no nutritional value. Serve soda as a special-occasion treat.
- *Bagels.* Bagels are an easy-to-prepare breakfast food for preschoolers, but a standard 6-inch bagel constitutes almost half of the recommended number of daily servings of grain for your

preschooler. Instead, opt for mini bagels, toast, or serve half of a bagel with a side of fresh fruit and yogurt. Also, bagels differ in density, so make sure that the bagel you give your child will crumble easily in their little mouths and not cause a choking hazard.

Favorite Foods

It's common for preschoolers to have a particular food that they just can't get enough of. Peanut butter and jelly sandwiches, macaroni and cheese, and chicken nuggets seem to be at the top of preschoolers' lists. But because healthy growth is a solid indicator of good eating habits, it's important to encourage your preschooler to eat a variety of different foods. Offer fresh fruits and vegetables, yogurt, and cheese along with their favorites and encourage your preschooler to try new, wholesome foods.

51 Stature and Weight Guidelines for Preschoolers

During the preschool years, weight gain slows. You can expect your preschooler to gain, on average, less than ½ pound per month. During these years, your child will, on average, gain about 5 pounds per year.[4] By 3 years of age, your preschooler may measure around 37 inches, your 4 year old, 40 inches, and your 5 year old, 42½ inches.[5]

2 to 20 years: Boys
Stature-for-age and Weight-for-age percentiles

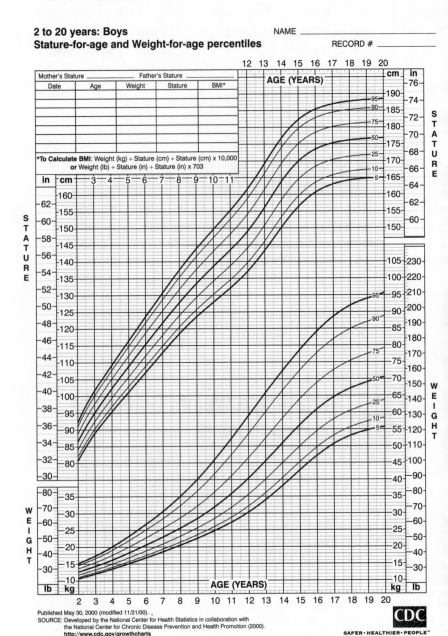

Published May 30, 2000 (modified 11/21/00).
SOURCE: Developed by the National Center for Health Statistics in collaboration with
the National Center for Chronic Disease Prevention and Health Promotion (2000).
http://www.cdc.gov/growthcharts

SAFER · HEALTHIER · PEOPLE™

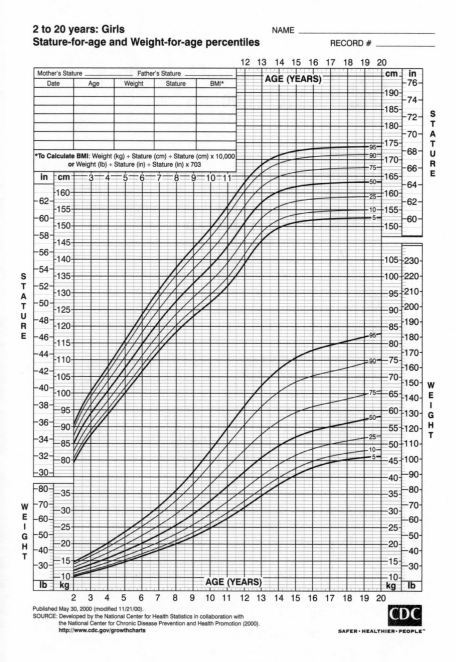

2 to 20 years: Girls
Stature-for-age and Weight-for-age percentiles

NAME _____

RECORD # _____

Published May 30, 2000 (modified 11/21/00).
SOURCE: Developed by the National Center for Health Statistics in collaboration with
the National Center for Chronic Disease Prevention and Health Promotion (2000).
http://www.cdc.gov/growthcharts

CDC
SAFER · HEALTHIER · PEOPLE™

177

▮▮▮▮ Developmental Milestones
52 for Preschoolers

Although it's impossible to tell exactly when a child will learn a specific skill, there are general milestones that can be used to gauge the developmental level of your preschooler. Don't panic if your child doesn't reach these milestones; instead, speak with your child's pediatrician about your concerns.

By the End of 48 Months/4 Years

Physical

Most children can:

✓ properly use utensils
✓ dress themselves
✓ hop on one foot
✓ jump over objects 5–6 inches high
✓ run, hop, skip, and jump around objects
✓ stack ten or more blocks
✓ catch and throw a ball

Intellectual

Most children can:

✓ sort objects from largest to smallest
✓ recognize letters
✓ print name if taught
✓ recognize familiar words

✓ understand concepts like biggest, tallest, more, same, under, over, in
✓ count up to seven objects aloud
✓ speak in complex sentences
✓ ask and answer questions starting with *who*, *what*, *when*, *where*, and *why*
✓ name six colors
✓ name several shapes
✓ follow two simple, unrelated sets of instructions

Social and Emotional

Most children can:

✓ take turns
✓ share
✓ have a conversation
✓ change the rules of games as they play
✓ understand simple rules
✓ constantly ask why
✓ tease and tattletale
✓ have trouble distinguishing fantasy from reality
✓ pretend elaborately in play

By the End of 60 Months/5 Years

Physical

Most children can:

✓ stand on one foot for at least 10 seconds
✓ do somersaults
✓ climb
✓ swing

✓ draw shapes by copying
✓ care for toileting needs independently
✓ print lots of letters
✓ dress and undress unassisted
✓ draw an identifiable person with a body

Intellectual
Most children can:

✓ count ten or more objects
✓ name lots of colors
✓ understand the concept of time
✓ know about money
✓ identify danger
✓ recall parts of stories

Social and Emotional
Most children can:

✓ say their name, address, and phone number
✓ try to please friends
✓ try to fit in with peers
✓ follow house and preschool rules
✓ identify differences in gender
✓ use future tense when speaking
✓ tell long stories

Is Your Child Ready for Preschool?

If you can answer yes to these eight questions, your child may benefit and enjoy attending a quality preschool program.

1. Is your child independent?
2. Does your child do well being away from you for long periods of time?
3. Can she complete small arts and crafts projects with minimal assistance?
4. Is she completely potty trained?
5. Does she do well in groups of other children?
6. Is she used to being on a regular schedule?
7. Can she physically and emotionally handle an entire day of play?
8. Is she used to taking only one afternoon nap?

53 The Preschooler's Library

Before children can read, they need to learn how to process the print on the pages of books. Exposing your preschooler to a variety of books, and reading to him often, not only fosters a love of books in your child, but can help him learn to recognize letters, become familiar with sounds of speech, and become aware of phonics, the foundational building blocks of reading.

Great books for the preschooler's library include:

1. *The Very Hungry Caterpillar* by Eric Carle
2. *Goodnight Moon* by Margaret Wise Brown
3. *The Runaway Bunny* by Margaret Wise Brown
4. *Brown Bear, Brown Bear, What Do You See?* by Bill Martin Jr.
5. *The Rainbow Fish* by Marcus Pfister
6. *Corduroy* by Don Freeman
7. *The Snowy Day* by Ezra Jack Keats

8. *Guess How Much I Love You* by Sam McBratney
9. *Good Dog, Carl* by Alexandra Day
10. *Good Night, Gorilla* by Peggy Rathmann
11. *How Do Dinosaurs Say Goodnight?* by Jane Yolen
12. *No, David!* by David Shannon
13. *We're Going on a Bear Hunt* by Helen Oxenbury
14. *Chicka Chicka Boom Boom* by Bill Martin Jr., John Archambault, and Lois Ehlert
15. *There Was an Old Lady Who Swallowed a Fly* by Simms Taback
16. *If You Give a Mouse a Cookie* by Laura Joffe Numeroff
17. *Cloudy with a Chance of Meatballs* by Judi Barret
18. *Richard Scarry's What People Do All Day* by Richard Scarry
19. *Dr. Seuss's ABC: An Amazing Alphabet Book!* by Dr. Seuss
20. *Where the Wild Things Are* by Maurice Sendak
21. *Who Is Jesus?* by Kathleen Bostrom
22. *What Is Prayer?* by Kathleen Bostrom
23. *What about Heaven?* by Kathleen Bostrom
24. *God Loves You* by Kathleen Bostrom
25. *God Gave Us You* by Lisa Tawn Bergren
26. *God Gave Us Christmas* by Lisa Tawn Bergren
27. *I Can Talk with God* by Debbie Anderson
28. *Punchinello and the Most Marvelous Gift* by Max Lucado
29. *If I Only Had a Green Nose* by Max Lucado
30. *You Are Special* by Max Lucado
31. *What to Expect at Preschool* by Heidi Eisenberg Murkoff and Laura Rader

Fostering a Love of Reading

By age 4, your child is well on his way to developing his prereading skills. These skills include recognizing print in various media, distinguishing separate words, recognizing words that rhyme, knowing some letter names and shapes, pretending to read, developing an understanding of simple stories, and recognizing his own name in print. Encourage a love of reading by taking time each day to read with your child. Start out by reading for just a few minutes. By age 4, your child should have the attention span for a 20-minute block of reading time per day.

54 Great DVDs for Preschoolers

Quality and *quantity* are the key words when it comes to television programming for your preschooler. The American Academy of Pediatrics recommends that television viewing for preschoolers be limited to 2 hours of quality programming per day.

While a variety of television stations offer nonstop programming for kids, DVDs are often a better choice for families of preschoolers because parents have more control over viewing time and program quality. With DVDs, commercials are eliminated and there is no need to schedule your preschooler's day around a favorite program or to delay bedtime until a show is over.

Top Picks

Scholastic Video Collection. This collection of DVDs features animated adaptations of kids' favorite stories. The DVDs display illustrated pages of the book as the words of the story are read. Some of the books that are featured include *How Do Dinosaurs Say Goodnight*, *Where the Wild Things Are*, *Make Way for Ducklings*, *Harold and the Purple Crayon*, and many, many more.

PBS Kids Programming. Children's favorite PBS television shows, like *Clifford the Big Red Dog, Arthur, Mr. Rogers, Sesame Street, and Thomas the Tank Engine* are available in DVD format for home viewing.

VeggieTales. This computer animated video series stars Bob the Tomato and Larry the Cucumber. Seen on the little and big screen, VeggieTales present Bible-based moral lessons and values. Some of the DVD video titles include *Where Is God When I'm S-Scared?* and *Larry Boy and the Rumor Weed*. Full-length feature films available on DVD include *Jonah: A VeggieTales Movie* and *The Pirates That Don't Do Anything: A VeggieTales Movie*.

Chronicles of Narnia: The Lion, the Witch, and the Wardrobe. This animated version of the C. S. Lewis classic children's book is perfect for the preschool audience. Unlike the Hollywood version of the classic, this animated adaptation won't scare the kids and they won't miss the message.

The Wiggles. Australia's favorite children's performers have made it big singing and dancing their way into the hearts of preschoolers. Their DVD series, including *Dance Party*, *Wiggle Time*, and *Wiggledancing*, will get your preschoolers moving and grooving to age-appropriate songs.

Ten Movies the Whole Family Can Enjoy

These are the Top Ten Movies for Family Audiences from the 17th Annual Faith and Values Awards Gala, sponsored by the Christian Film & Television Commission.

1. Wall-E
2. Fireproof

3. The Chronicles Of Narnia: Prince Caspian
4. Bolt
5. Journey To The Center Of The Earth 3d
6. Nim's Island
7. Kung Fu Panda
8. The Tale Of Despereaux
9. Madagascar: Escape 2 Africa
10. High School Musical 3: Senior Year[6]

Plugged In Online

Plugged In Online (www.pluggedinonline.com) is a Focus on the Family website that provides detailed entertainment reviews that families can use to determine if a movie is acceptable for their viewing.

55 The Preschooler's Playroom

Preschoolers are the masters of make-believe, so any realistic toys that promote role-playing will be a sure hit. Look for toys that engage your child, rather than offer only electronic entertainment. Toys that provide an opportunity for your preschooler to express creativity and to master new skills will be most enjoyed.

barn
cash register
doctor bag
dollhouse
little people and animals

play kitchen
pretend foods
tool sets
train and train track on a
train table

card games
magnetic fishing game
matching games
puzzles with twenty to fifty
    pieces
simple board games

musical instruments
toy keyboard or piano

ride-on toys
tricycle

gym sets
soccer ball
softball and bat

learning bank
learning clock
smaller Legos

easel
felt board
lacing cards
puppets
puppet theater

Melissa & Doug

"From puzzles to puppets, plush to play food, magnetic activities, music, and more, Melissa & Doug is one of the leading designers and manufacturers of educational toys and children's products. Started in 1988 in their garage, Melissa & Doug has something for everyone, with nearly eight hundred unique and exciting products for children of all ages!"[7]

Setting up the Playroom

When setting up your preschooler's play area, utilize a bin system to keep things organized. Allocate a bin for each type of toy that your child has—one for small cars, one for instruments, one for farm animals, one for play food, one for blocks, and so on. Print the category on the bin or cut out photos of the type of toy that the bin holds and attach it to the front of the bin. Not only will this help keep the toys organized, it will *make for easy cleanup that your preschooler can manage herself.*

▮▮▮▮ Ten Awesome Activities
56 for Preschoolers

Preschoolers love hands-on activities that allow them to explore their world. Activities that engage their senses and provide an opportunity to learn something new will be a huge success. Try out these ten awesome activities with your preschooler.

Making Salt Art

Materials

newspaper
salt
colored chalk
clear glass baby food jar with cover

Instructions

1. Lay newspaper over the work area.
2. Pour salt onto the newspaper, a separate pile for each color you want to create (probably several teaspoons each, depending on how many jars you want to make).
3. Roll selected color of chalk over one pile of salt, until salt reaches desired color.
4. Repeat with as many different colors as desired.

5. Layer the different colors of salt in the glass jar using a spoon.
6. Place the lid on the jar.

Making Stained Glass Butterflies

Materials

wax paper	iron
crayons	hole punch
crayon sharpener	yarn or string
small towel	

Instructions

1. Fold a piece of wax paper in half to make a crease. Unfold.
2. Starting at the crease, draw half of a butterfly on one side.
3. Repeat on the other side of the crease.
4. Use the crayon sharpener to create various colors of crayon shavings.
5. Arrange the crayon shavings on the wax paper, inside the outline of butterfly's wings.
6. Place a second piece of wax paper on top of the shaving-filled butterfly.
7. Place a small towel on top of the wax paper.
8. Have an adult iron the wax paper together on low heat.
9. Allow the wax paper to cool.
10. Cut out the butterfly.
11. Punch a hole near the top of the butterfly.
12. Tie a string through the hole.
13. Hang the butterfly in a window.

Making a Bird Feeder

Materials

string	bowl
pinecone	birdseed
creamy peanut butter	

Instructions

1. Tie a piece of string to the stem of a pinecone.
2. Spread peanut butter all over the pinecone.
3. Fill a bowl with birdseed.
4. Roll the pinecone in the seed.
5. Hang the pinecone from a tree branch.

Going on Animal Adventures

Many local pet stores, farms, and zoos allow children to interact with their animals. Some farms and zoos even allow children to participate in caring for the animals. Most preschoolers enjoy observing, petting, and feeding animals, so a trip to a place where they can do this will make for an exciting adventure.

Going for a Nature Walk

Preschoolers like to collect things, and a nature walk provides the perfect opportunity for a child to collect leaves, small twigs, or flowers. These collections can later be used for an arts and crafts project.

Playing Hide the Bones

While you can really use anything to hide, small plastic bones fascinate preschoolers. Visit your local party supply store and purchase a few bags of small plastic bones (or any other small plastic toy). Have your preschooler cover his eyes while you hide the bones. Although this game can be played indoors or out, outside play of this game may inspire your child to pretend he's a fascinating character, like an archeologist searching for dinosaur bones. Give him a shovel and bucket to help him with his hide-and-seek mission.

Playing with Oobleck

Materials

Bartholomew and the Oobleck by Dr. Seuss
bowl
2 cups of cornstarch
green food coloring
1 cup of water

Instructions

1. Read *Bartholomew and the Oobleck* by Dr. Seuss.
2. Place cornstarch in a bowl.
3. Add green food coloring.
4. Add water.
5. Mix.
6. Experiment with moving the Oobleck around in the bowl. When you move it fast it behaves like a solid, but when you move it slow it behaves like a liquid.

Making a Hand Wreath

Materials

paper	scissors
paint	glue

Instructions

1. Dip hand in paint and make twelve handprints on paper.
2. Let dry.
3. Cut out handprints.
4. Glue hand cutouts together, overlapping at the wrists, to form a circle.
5. Add more decoration by drawing and cutting out a paper ribbon and ornaments and gluing them to the wreath.

Making Homemade Applesauce

Materials

Crock-Pot   potato masher

Ingredients

8 apples, cored, peeled, and sliced
½ cup of water
¾ cup brown sugar
1 teaspoon cinnamon

Instructions

1. Go apple picking or purchase apples from your local grocer.
2. Combine all ingredients in the Crock-Pot.
3. Turn Crock-Pot on high.
4. When apples are soft (about 3 to 4 hours), use potato masher to mash the apples into sauce.

Creating a Color Scratch

Materials

paper   crayons   spoon

Instructions

1. Color stripes of various colors on the paper.
2. Color over the entire page with black crayon.
3. Use the end of a spoon to "scratch" a picture through the black crayon. You'll expose the original colors underneath.

The Preschooler's Arts and Crafts Pantry*

contact paper
easel paper
paper, assorted
    colors, sizes,
    and textures
tissue paper
waxed paper

chalk
children's scissors
colored pencils
crayons
crayon sharpener
hole punch
markers
pencils
pencil sharpener

paintbrushes,
    assorted
tempera paints

watercolor paints

glue
glue stick
stapler
tape

baby food jars
birdseed
buttons, assorted
    shapes, sizes,
    and colors
catalogs
cotton balls
felt
glitter
old socks
paper lunch bags
paper plates
paper towel rolls
pasta noodles

pipe cleaners   sponges
Popsicle sticks   straws
sand   yarn

*When children are using these items, close adult su-
pervision is required!

57 Six Steps to a Successful Preschool Playdate

Playdates provide a wonderful opportunity for children to play with others and practice their social skills, but if a playdate isn't carefully planned out, it can be a recipe for disaster. Follow these steps for planning the perfect playdate.

1. *Prepare in advance.* Set up the time and the environment for a win-win situation. Work around nap times, limit playdates to two hours, and childproof the areas you'll be using. The ideal number of children for a playdate is the age of your child plus one, although playdates with larger groups can be successful with a little extra planning and preparation.
2. *Make sharing easier.* Put away any special toys that your child doesn't like to share. Every child should have a few toys that are "off limits" to others. Putting these prized possessions away during playdates can head off potential sharing problems.
3. *Set up stations.* In the play area, set up a few different stations for the children to play in. Activities that several children can participate in at the same time work best for group play. A station for blocks, one for kitchen play,

and one for games (like Hullabaloo or Simon Says) will keep larger groups of kids actively engaged.

4. *Serve a snack*. Having a light snack—fresh fruit, cheese, and milk—on hand can provide the perfect break if things get tense.

5. *Explain the ground rules*. Let kids know the rules before playtime starts. For example: "We play in this room, we keep our hands to ourselves, and we use our indoor voices." Spelling out your expectations can eliminate blurry boundaries.

6. *Allow the children to work out their own problems*. Let the children play and learn to work out minor squabbles on their own. Unless it gets physical or emotionally hurtful, allowing kids to solve their disputes is the best way to foster communication, negotiation, and social skills.

Playdate Themes

Having a theme for your playdate can make things super fun, and providing a loose structure for the playtime helps make it successful. "On the Farm" and "In the Kitchen" are great playdate themes. Collect and put out all of the toys and books that you have related to your theme, make copies of coloring pages that depict your theme, and serve a snack that reflects the theme.

58 Teaching Children to Share Step-by-Step

Sharing is a learned skill that develops over time and is usually mastered in the early elementary school years. Parents can help their preschoolers learn how to share by encouraging sharing, modeling sharing, and providing opportunities for preschoolers to practice sharing.

Step 1: Set the Ground Rules

The ground rules for sharing should include:

- Always ask to use something that doesn't belong to you.
- Say more than no if someone asks to play with your toy. You can decline and choose not to share but you must offer an alternative, such as taking turns, suggesting a different toy, or giving a specific reason for saying no.
- Treat others as you would like to be treated.

Step 2: Encourage Sharing

- Read books about sharing.
- Talk about sharing.
- Provide opportunities to play in groups.
- Play games that require turns to be taken.
- Praise your child when she shares.

Step 3: Model Sharing

- Share things with your child.
- Point out when you notice other people sharing and name it as such.
- Role-play sharing with your child and spouse.

Don't Force Your Preschooler to Share Everything

Every preschooler has a few toys to which she has a strong emotional connection. These toys should be given special status, and your child should not be forced to share them. Discourage your child from bringing these toys to play groups or child care. In group settings it can be overwhelming to a child if other children want to play with her prized possession. If your child insists on bringing the favorite toy out during a playdate, be firm about putting it away if sharing becomes a problem. If you will not be there, let the adult in charge know to put the toy in her backpack (or with her coat) should it become a problem.

59 Twenty-five Great Places to Take Preschool-age Children

Most preschoolers love being out and about, and outings provide opportunities for your child to explore her world, release her energy, and discover new things. Outings can also help to channel your preschooler's energy and make your caretaking responsibilities more enjoyable. Here are some great places to go:

1. playground
2. library
3. zoo
4. farm
5. pet store
6. aquarium
7. children's museum

8. indoor play space
9. age-appropriate puppet show, musical, or theatrical performance
10. beach or lake
11. state park
12. indoor pool
13. ice-skating rink
14. the local fire station
15. the local police station
16. age-appropriate theme or amusement park
17. apple orchard
18. train ride
19. play group
20. nature education center
21. art museum
22. pick-your-own fruit or veggie patch
23. bookstore
24. paint-your-own pottery shop
25. kids' gym

Packing for a Day Out with Your Preschooler

Being prepared should be your motto when heading out and about with your preschooler. On any day trip, be sure to take along the following:

- snacks
- drinks
- change of clothes
- sunscreen
- wet wipes
- bottled water
- first aid kit
- camera

60 Classes Preschoolers Really Enjoy

The preschool years are a time of tremendous social, emotional, and physical development. During these years, preschool children begin to take a real interest in themselves, their environment, and the people around them. Preschool classes provide an opportunity for children to interact with their peers, learn to function in a group, understand the role of a teacher, and learn through play in a stimulating, age-appropriate environment.

And since most homes of preschoolers aren't equipped to provide safe environments dedicated to specific, specialized activities for small children, you and your preschooler may enjoy the following types of classes. However, while classes may be fun and educational, it's best to limit enrollment to no more than two classes per week.

Top Ten Classes for Preschoolers

1. Sunday school classes
2. gymnastics classes
3. music classes
4. dance classes
5. art classes
6. cooking classes
7. swim classes*
8. karate classes
9. sports classes
10. language classes

*Many preschoolers love the water, but until your preschooler is around 4 years old, he won't be developmentally ready for formal swimming lessons.[8] Before then, enrolling preschoolers in a mommy-and-me type of swim class can help a child become familiar with the water and can help him learn about water safety.

Top Picks

Sunday School Classes

Sunday school classes can make Bible stories come to life for your child. With fun, age-appropriate activities, preschoolers can learn Bible basics through classroom instruction, craft projects, songs, and skits. Sunday school classes offer great reinforcement of the values and beliefs you teach your child at home.

Gymnastics Classes

Gymnastics classes provide a safe opportunity for children to climb, jump, and swing away their energy. Classes for preschoolers provide an outlet for kids to work on motor skills, coordination, and balance in a fun and stimulating environment. A good kids' gym will focus on growth and development through exercise, games, music and movement, and sports. It will not foster intense competition among young children.

Music Classes

Preschoolers love music and what better way to let them experience it than playing their own? Music classes provide an opportunity for young children to explore a variety of musical styles and to sing, play, and dance to their own beat. Children who are regularly engaged in musical moments "do better in reading and math when they start school, are better able to focus and control their bodies, play better with others, and have higher self-esteem."[9]

Kids' Gyms with Franchises across the United States

Gymboree
The Little Gym
My Gym
Romp n' Roll
Kids U

Family Favorite

A good preschool music class will not be performance based, but instead will focus on the musical experience of the child. Music Together (www.musictogether.com) is an internationally recognized music program for young children and their families. Their classes provide a positive introduction to music and give children an opportunity to explore music through song, dance, and movement.

When Choosing a Class for Your Preschooler

- Look for a class that focuses on experience rather than performance.
- Choose classes that have instructors who are certified or credentialed in the field they are teaching.
- Pick classes that have teachers experienced in working with preschoolers.
- Opt for classes specifically designed for preschoolers.
- Choose classes that have an open-door policy regarding parent observation.

Free Finds

Many libraries and community centers offer free classes for preschoolers. Usually you can find no-cost classes advertised in your local newspaper calendar section, at your community library, or in dedicated community family and kids publications. Your local YMCA or community center may also offer scholarships for classes to children of families in financial need.

61 Marks of a *Great* Preschool

For children ages 3 to 5, preschool can be a positive first introduction to the classroom. In addition to academic fundamentals, preschool provides an opportunity for children to develop important social skills. Preschool allows children to learn to interact and play with others, interact with a teacher, wait and take turns, and listen and follow instructions.

Components of a *Great* Preschool Program

an understanding that kids learn through play

happy kids that look forward to going to school

a variety of activities for children to participate in, including blocks, puzzles, arts and crafts, and props for pretend

a structured day that allows for circle time, outside time, playtime, rest time, and snack time

201

lots of picture books for reading and storybooks that are read to children individually and in groups

toys that are organized and arranged in a way that promotes play

a well-trained staff (and low staff turnover) who interact with children in groups and individually

appropriate licenses and accreditations

a teacher-to-student ratio of no more than ten preschool-age children per teacher[10]

a good reputation in the community

a curriculum that allows children to learn at their own pace

clearly communicated policies and procedures as well as a learning philosophy that meshes with yours

Before Signing Up Your Child

- *Do your research.* Know what type of philosophy the program embraces and determine if that philosophy best suits the needs of your child. A preschool that is rooted in the group-oriented Waldorf philosophy may be better for some children, while the Montessori style of individualized education may be best for others.
- *Start your search early.* Often quality programs have long waiting lists (read: *years!*) so it's important that you reserve a slot in your favorite program as soon as possible.
- *Visit with and without your child.* You'll want to be sure that the school practices what it preaches and that your child feels comfortable in the environment.
- *Interview your child's potential teacher.* You'll want to have a clear understanding of who your child's teacher would be, her classroom expectations, and what her style of teaching is.

The Importance of NAEYC Accreditation

The National Association for the Education of Young Children offers a voluntary accreditation program for preschools. Programs that have been accredited by the NAEYC meet the standards of excellence that the association has established for health, safety, and education. To find a NAEYC accredited program in your area, visit www.naeyc.org.

62 Ten Practical Christian Principles to Teach Your Preschooler

Chances are, during the preschool years, your child will have her first lengthy experiences with other children and adults away from the safety of you and your home. For some families, this will be the first time that their child is exposed to a non-Christian worldview. To world-proof your preschooler, it's vital that your child have a basic understanding of Christian beliefs. Instill the following ten Christian principles to live by in your preschooler.

1. *God is good all the time* (see Ps. 100:5). In a world where bad things happen, it's important that your preschooler know that God is good. Teach your child that regardless of the way things appear, we can trust in the goodness of God.
2. *God made the world and everything in it* (see Gen. 1). It's more common than ever for schools to teach evolution rather than creationism. Teach your child that God is the creator and maker of all.

203

3. *We are* all *created in the image of God* (see Gen. 1:27). Kids can be mean to other children who look different. They can tease, taunt, and terrorize them. Protect your preschooler from peer pressure by preparing her to reject the invitations to join in such abuse. Teach your child that God made everyone in his image, and no one should ever be teased for how he looks.

4. *Boys marry girls, and girls marry boys* (see Mark 10:6–8). In an age when gay marriage is legal in some states, it's important to teach your child that God created woman for man and man for woman. When your preschooler comes home and proudly announces that Sarah has two mommies, and she wants two too, one way you can gently address the issue is by saying that in your family, you believe in the Bible and the Bible says that girls are supposed to marry boys. Phrasing your information like this moves the focus from what Sarah's parents are doing "wrong" to what is acceptable in your family's moral code. It also directs your child back to the basis of your belief system—the Bible—rather than leaving her to believe it's just your opinion.

5. *God has a good and special plan for your life* (see Jer. 29:11).The pressure to fit in is high, even among preschoolers, and sometimes a child's self-esteem can suffer because of it. Teach your child that God knows her, loves her, and has a good plan for her.

6. *Put Jesus first* (see Luke 10:38–42). Preschoolers are learning to make choices and to be independent. Teach your child to put Jesus first by being a "What would Jesus do?" role model. Allow your child to see you pray, ask God for help, and make choices that glorify him.

7. *God hears our prayers* (see Luke 11:9). Sometimes kids feel that no one is listening to them. Teach your child that she can always talk to God and God always listens.

8. *The condition of the heart is what matters* (see 1 Sam. 16:6–7). God cares about the inside of our hearts. Teach your child the value of being honest, loving, and kind. Be a role model and offer your child praise when you notice he's performed an act of kindness or told the truth when it was hard.

9. *God loves everybody* (see John 3:16). Teach your child that everyone is special to God and that he wants everyone to be part of his family.

10. *Jesus is the only way to heaven* (see John 14:6). During the preschool years, your child may hear about "other" ways to get to heaven. Root your child in the truth and teach your preschooler that Jesus is the only way, the truth, and the light. When your child comes home and tells you she thinks she can get to heaven just by being a good person, like her friend says, gently explain that people believe in different things and it's our job to love them like Jesus does and pray that they will know Jesus as their Savior and Friend.

But if SHE Can Do It, Why Can't I?

When teaching Christian principles to your preschooler, it's important to instill your beliefs without putting others down. Often preschoolers aren't able to understand in-depth theological concepts and can twist your lengthy explanations into something you didn't mean. Focus on what your family believes and practices, rather than on how others live. This can help to avoid sending your child the message that we are "good" and others are "bad."

63 Teaching Your Preschooler to Pray

We often teach our children that they can always talk to God, but sometimes we don't teach them how. While there is no formula that we have to follow to engage God in conversation, we can help our children develop good prayer habits by teaching them some biblical principles concerning prayer.

ACTS Prayer Model for Kids

Many new believers learn to pray following the ACTS (adoration, confession, thanksgiving, and supplication) model of prayer, and this model can be easily adapted for young children to understand.

Big Words	Little Words
adoration	I love you! You're great!
confession	I'm sorry. I messed up.
thanksgiving	Thank you.
supplication	Please.

A Child's Prayer

God, I love you! You are great!
I'm sorry I didn't listen to my mom.
Thank you for my family.
Please help me to be a better listener.

The Lord's Prayer

Most churchgoing preschoolers are familiar with the Lord's Prayer. They may have even learned to say it in Sunday school. To help your child understand the Lord's Prayer, break down its meaning line-by-line.

> Our Father which art in heaven, Hallowed by thy name. Thy kingdom come, thy will be done in earth, as it is in heaven. Give us this day our daily bread. And forgive us our debts, as we forgive our debtors. And lead us not into temptation, but deliver us from evil: For thine is the kingdom, and the power, and the glory, for ever. Amen.
>
> Matthew 6:9–13 KJV

The Lord's Prayer

Verse	What It Means
Our Father, which art in heaven	Tells us that we are praying to God, our heavenly Father
Hallowed by thy name	Tells us God is holy
thy kingdom come	We're asking God to let us share in his kingdom
thy will be done in earth, as it is in heaven	We're asking to do what God wants us to do
Give us this day our daily bread	We're asking and trusting God to give us what we need
And forgive us our debts, as we forgive our debtors	We're asking God to forgive us for the bad things we've done and we're telling God we've forgiven others who have done bad things to us
And lead us not into temptation, but deliver us from evil	We're asking God to help us do the right thing and stay out of trouble
For thine is the kingdom, and the power, and the glory, for ever	We're acknowledging that everything belongs to God forever, and we're saying we know that God can answer our prayers
Amen	We're asking God to hear and trusting him to answer our prayer

⬛⬛⬛ Recommended Resources for
64 Mothers of Preschoolers

Organizations

MOPS International—www.mops.org

Mothers of Preschoolers International (MOPS) is an organization designed to support *all* mothers of preschoolers. Moms of preschoolers can get in-person support by attending a local MOPS group. They can also glean valuable information and access resources from the MOPS website.

NAEYC—www.naeyc.org

The National Association for the Education of Young Children (NAEYC) is "dedicated to improving the well-being of all young children, with particular focus on the quality of educational and developmental services for all children from birth through age eight."[11] NAEYC is an especially valuable organization for parents who are exploring early childhood education options.

ACSI—www.acsi.org

The Association of Christian Schools International (ACSI) can help you locate an evangelical, Protestant, Christian early education program near you.

Books

801 Questions Kids Ask about God: With Answers from the Bible
produced by Lightwave and Livingstone

Ask Supernanny: What Every Parent Wants to Know by Jo Frost

Chicken Soup for the Mothers of Preschooler's Soul: Stories to Refresh the Soul and Rekindle the Spirit of Moms of Little Ones by Mark Victor Hansen, Jack Canfield, Maria Nickless, and Elisa Morgan

Nanny 911: Expert Advice for All of Your Parenting Emergencies by Deborah Carroll and Stella Reid

Nanny to the Rescue! Straight Talk and Super Tips for Parenting in the Early Years by Michelle LaRowe

The One Year Book of Devotions for Preschoolers by Crystal Bowman and Elena Kucharik

LISTS FOR FAMILY AND FRIENDS

65 Ten House Rules for Every Home

Every family has a set of unique house rules, whether they're expressed or not. House rules are the nonnegotiable rules of the family. They work to create a smoothly operating family environment.

When creating your house rules, use this list as your guide:

1. Keep your hands to yourself
2. Use kind words
3. Always tell the truth
4. Listen to and obey your parents
5. No means no
6. Use your indoor voice
7. Age-appropriate toys and TV only
8. Take care of your belongings
9. Pick up after yourself
10. Ask before using things that are not yours

Making Your House Rules Effective

House rules are most effective when:

- all family members have a clear understanding of what the rules are.
- all family members make a conscious agreement to follow them.

- all adults in the home make a commitment to consistently enforce them.

66 Bully Proofing Your Kids

According to the National Youth Violence Prevention Resource Center, nearly 30 percent of all American youth are affected by bullying.[1] Webster's dictionary defines bullying as "treating one in an overbearing or intimidating manner."

Kids bully for many reasons. Some of these reasons are to exert control, as a result of peer pressure, and out of a misguided attempt to increase self-esteem. Regardless of the reason, bullying is never acceptable. And bullying isn't limited to boys. While boys may engage in physical bullying, girls will often tease and exclude their classmates, which is a form of emotional bullying.

To bully proof your kid, follow these steps:

1. Talk to your child about bullying. Let your child know that you're aware bullying happens.
2. Encourage him to come to you if he is being bullied. Let him know that you are committed to taking his reports seriously.
3. Observe your child for signs that he's being bullied. Notice changes of behavior in your child. Pay attention if he seems suddenly withdrawn or anxious.
4. Keep the lines of communication open. Make it a policy to talk to your child each day about his experiences. Ask open-ended questions and probe deeper if you sense that something is wrong.

5. Teach your child the following effective techniques for dealing with bullies.

Teach your child to:

- pretend that the comments don't bother him
- ignore the bully's tactics
- avoid the bully
- assert himself by saying, "Stop! I don't like it!"
- have strong body language that displays self-confidence
- ask the bully why he would say something so hurtful
- use "I want" statements, like "I want you to stop calling me names"
- use humor by saying, "Wow, that was a good one!" with a chuckle
- tell an adult

Role-play bullying scenarios with your child, using the tools above to help empower and prepare him for dealing with a bully.

Tips to Avoid Raising a Bully

Teach your child to respect all people.
Encourage an empathetic spirit.
Set clear guidelines for how to treat people.
Use nonviolent disciplinary methods.
Have a no-tolerance policy for bullying.

The Dos and Don'ts of Bullying

Do: Believe your child.
Do: Build up your child's self-esteem.

Do: Gather all of the facts.

Do: Foster your child's friendships.

Don't: Blame your child.

Don't: Promise you won't tell anyone.

Don't: Confront the bully or parents of the bully by yourself. Instead, do so with a school principal or other authority figure.

67 Selecting a Family-Friendly Church

Marriage, relocation, and other life circumstances can make finding a new home church necessary. Although a church doesn't have to have a full-blown children's ministry to be family friendly, there are certain characteristics and services that are essential. When shopping for a new church, use this checklist to evaluate the family friendliness of the church you're visiting.

Yes No

☐☐ There is a nursery to care for babies or young children during the service.

☐☐ There is a quiet place to nurse or feed a baby.

☐☐ There is a director of children's ministries.

☐☐ There is an established ministry for children.

☐☐ There is a children's church service.

☐☐ Children are regularly involved in the worship service.

☐☐ The pastor hosts a children's time during the service.

☐☐ There are coloring pages or books provided for children during the service.

☐☐ There is child care provided during church events.

☐☐ There is a system in place for signing children in and out of classes.

☐☐ The rooms children use are clean and bright.

☐☐ There are child-size tables and chairs in the classrooms.

☐☐ There are changing tables in the bathrooms.

☐☐ Volunteer workers are thoroughly screened.

☐☐ Volunteers are trained.

☐☐ There is an active youth group.

☐☐ There is children's artwork displayed in the church.

☐☐ The church hosts vacation Bible school.

☐☐ There are church security measures in place.

☐☐ The church holds social events for families.

☐☐ The church has parenting resources available.

☐☐ Many families attend the church.

☐☐ The church hosts support groups.

☐☐ Pictures of church events are displayed and families are included.

☐☐ The church has a MOPS (Mothers of Preschoolers) group.

LIST

68 Feeding a Picky Eater

At one time or another, every mother is parent to the world's pickiest eater. If you're sick of serving up the same ol' stuff, try these tips for introducing new foods to toddlers and preschoolers.

- *Serve small portions, in small pieces, in small spaces.* An ice cube tray filled with colorful cut ups in each compartment is a great way to present a combination of new foods and old favorites in a nonintimidating way.
- *Dip into dips.* Cottage cheese, yogurt, cream cheese, and peanut butter make for great fruit and veggie dips. When it comes to meat, ketchup covers a multitude of unforgiving smells, textures, and appearances.
- *Let your child feed herself.* Presenting any new selection in a finger friendly way will increase the chances that your child will try it.
- *Prepare it differently.* A child who doesn't like the texture of crispy raw carrots may love them steamed and soft.
- *Slow and steady.* Less is more when introducing new, exotic, or ethnic spices.
- *Color your food.* Food coloring can dynamically impact the attractiveness of a food. Add a few drops of food coloring to new foods and you may be surprised how eager your child is to try them. (Use strong colored veggie juice for a great all-natural alternative.)
- *Share a fork.* Kids will often be more eager to try something new if it comes from your plate.
- *Encourage turn taking.* Insist that your child try the new food before she eats her favorite food. Encourage her to take turns, taking a bite of the old favorite, followed by the new.
- *Keep it low-key.* Don't make a huge deal about serving up something new; instead, keep a nonchalant attitude that says, "This is just something else we eat."
- *Offer positive, purposeful praise.* Offering an "I'm really proud that you tried a bite!" goes a long way in promot-

ing an attitude of willingness when it comes to trying new foods.

- *Don't give up.* It can take on average eight times of being exposed to a new food before a child may even try it, never mind acquire a taste for it. Offer the same new food often, even if it was previously rejected.

Top Three Turnoffs

Children will often refuse to try a new food because of these top three turnoffs:

1. the way foods look
2. the way foods feel
3. the way foods smell

The Goal Is Trying

When it comes right down to it, introducing new foods is really about trying—not necessarily liking.

69 Age-Appropriate Chores for Young Children

Chores provide an opportunity for even the youngest member of the family to feel as if he is making a valuable contribution to the family unit. Chores facilitate a helping spirit and teach children the importance of teamwork. Although different children may be developmentally ready to pitch in at different times, the following chart can help you identify which tasks your child may be developmentally able to perform.

Age-Appropriate Chores for Children

2–3 Years	3–4 Years	4–5 Years
Put napkins on table	Carry light groceries from car	Set and clear table with minimal help
Help clear his plate from table	Put pantry food away	Help load and unload dishwasher
Clean up small spills	Help prepare food	Sort and fold laundry
Put clothes in the hamper	Help set and clear table	Help make bed
Match socks	Help take clothes out of dryer	Help put groceries away
Carry small piles of washcloths and towels	Help water plants	Vacuum with supervision
Dust with socks on hands	Water the garden	Sweep small areas
Feed pets with assistance	Put away toys independently	Empty wastebaskets
Put toys away in baskets	Put books on a shelf	Feed pets with supervision

More than Chores

Although it can be tempting to save time by completing household tasks yourself, resist the urge to do what your child is able to do. Chores teach basic life skills, such as responsibility and task completion, and can help instill a good work ethic in your child. In addition, allowing a child to do things that he is able to do for himself helps build his self-esteem and self-worth.

⬛⬛S⬛ Twenty Family Outings That
70 Are Fun for Everyone

For families with children of various ages, finding a one-size-fits-all family adventure can be hard. These twenty family-friendly outings can be fun for all ages.

1. *A trip to the zoo.* Put younger children in backpack carriers or strollers and allow older children to walk beside you.
2. *A day at the beach or lake.* Bring along an assortment of sand toys, balls, and kites to create fun for all ages.
3. *An afternoon of sledding.* Young children can be pulled along on a sled or they can play with the snow, while older siblings race down hills on sleds.
4. *A trip to the museum.* Many museums have exhibits geared toward different ages. Divide and conquer; then meet up for lunch.
5. *A day of hiking.* Take turns carrying young children in front carriers or backpacks and have older children take turns leading the way.
6. *A visit to a corn maze.* Split into teams and race to see who can find his or her way through the maze first.
7. *A trip to the farm.* Most kids love animals and if there's a petting zoo, it will be a sure hit for the entire family.
8. *A camping adventure.* Whether you're in your own backyard or on a campsite, camping is a great family activity. Fish, roast marshmallows, and sit around a campfire singing songs.
9. *Pick your own fruit or veggies.* This can be a daylong event. Younger children can help pick produce, and

221

older children can prepare a sweet treat with their fresh pickings after returning home.

10. *Attending an outdoor concert.* Music and dancing in the great outdoors can be fun for all ages. Make homemade instruments and take them along.

11. *Mini golfing.* Divide into teams so that adults can help younger children while older siblings manage on their own. Infants can be worn in a front carrier or backpack.

12. *Take a bike ride.* If you're an outdoorsy family, consider purchasing a bike trailer for hauling little ones.

13. *Bowling.* Many bowling alleys have inflatable gutter guards to prevent balls from going into the gutter. Kids as young as two can manage a ten-pin ball.

14. *A trip to the aquarium.* Many aquariums have discovery areas where children can have a hands-on aquatic experience. Some even host dolphin or sea lion shows that are entertaining for all ages.

15. *A trip to a homemade ice cream stand.* A trip to an old-fashioned dairy farm that makes its own ice cream is hard to pass up at any age.

16. *Visit to a state park.* A picnic basket, a blanket, a Wiffle bat and ball, and some inflatable beach balls will offer a variety of entertainment for all.

17. *Trip to a theme park.* A visit to a family-friendly theme park can be a great family adventure. Consider taking turns riding age-appropriate amusement rides with each child.

18. *Attend a circus.* Many families enjoy watching an old-fashioned circus. From animals to acrobats, kids of all ages will be entertained.

19. *Go to a family show.* Ice shows, puppet shows, and interactive children's theater are designed to capture the attention of a varied age group. Added bonus: you won't have to stress out about chatty kids.

20. *Do a drive-in movie.* Family movies on the big, big screen are a great alternative to the traditional theater. Go at nap time, if possible, so babies will sleep in their car seats while parents and older siblings enjoy the show. (Visit www.drive-ins.com to see if there is a drive-in movie theater in your area.)

71 Ten Tips for Traveling with Kids

Traveling with the kids takes a lot more planning than it did in your kid-free days. And if you're not prepared, you can be in for quite a challenge. To ensure that you'll be holding nonstop tickets to paradise, follow these ten tips.

1. *Plan in advance.* Research your travel options, accommodations, and destination before finalizing your travel plans.
2. *Pack purposely.* Less is more when traveling with kids. Plan on doing laundry while you're away; you'll cut down significantly on your baggage. You'll also want to avoid taking large items, which you can rent or borrow at your destination.
3. *Pack play bags for each child.* Fill a small backpack with snacks, drinks, books, and small toys or magnetic games for your child to play on the trip. A clipboard can be great for older children, serving as a lap desk on which to color or play word games.
4. *Place essential items in an easy-to-access location.* Be sure to pack medications, travel documents, changes of clothes, and other essential items in a carryall bag. Keep this bag within easy reach at all times.

5. *Pack plenty of drinks and snacks.* Take along lots of healthy snacks, like dried fruit, granola bars, or peanut butter and crackers, as well as kid-sized bottled waters or juice boxes. Often it can be hard to find your kid's favorites when traveling.

6. *Play on a schedule.* Sticking to your regular routine while away will make for a much more enjoyable trip. Keep mealtimes and sleep times regular while traveling to ensure that your children are well rested and that their blood sugar levels remain constant.

7. *Put safety first.* It can be hard not to bend the rules while you're away, but when it comes to safety, be a stickler. If you're traveling with a baby or toddler, consider taking along items to childproof your home away from home.

8. *Photograph everything.* Capture the memories of your trip by taking lots of photos. Consider compiling a vacation scrapbook when you return home.

9. *Plan breaks.* Set aside time for the kids to take a break. Plan to stop during long car rides, take breaks while you're at amusement parks, and schedule a daily time of rest during your travels.

10. *Pack your sense of humor.* You'll definitely need your sense of humor to survive a trip with kids in tow. Keep a lighthearted spirit and try not to get upset over the little bumps in your travel road.

Car Backseat Organizers

Car backseat trays and organizers are perfect travel companions for older kids. They provide a neat, easy, and accessible place to hold your child's car toys. Some even have a flip-down tray that gives kids a flat surface for eating or coloring (check out www.kidkase.com).

LIST
72 Items in a Well-Stocked Vehicle

Whether you're faced with a growling stomach or an exploding diaper, having a well-stocked vehicle can keep you out of a jam. Being prepared for potential problems can save you from having to cut your outing short or from making a pit stop at an all-too-expensive convenience store. It's also good to stock your vehicle with items that you may need in the case of a roadside emergency.

For Babies

a seasonal change of clothes

diapers

wet wipes

formula

bottled water

sippy cup

baby food

baby utensils

For Toddlers

a seasonal change of clothes

Pull-Ups

snacks

sippy cup

bottled water

100 percent fruit juice boxes

snack foods like dried fruit, granola bars, or crackers

an extra pair of shoes

For Older Children and Grown-ups

a seasonal change of
clothes
an extra pair of shoes

bottled water
snacks

For Cleanup

beach towel
paper towels

plastic bags
rags

For Safety

blanket
duct tape
extra car fuses
first aid kit
flashlight and batteries
"Help!" sign
ice scraper
jumper cables

map
paper
pen
pocket knife
roadside flares
tire inflator (such as Fix-
a-Flat)

Storing Your Supplies

A basket with handles, backpack, or other nylon bag
can be a great place to store your supplies. Store them
in the trunk of your vehicle, out of the reach of children.
Seat organizers that attach to the back of the driver's
seat can be handy for storing diapers, wipes, and other
baby care items.

AAA

An annual membership in AAA will most likely cost you less than a tow to your local garage if you were to need one. In addition to emergency roadside assistance, AAA membership provides access to free resources, like maps and trip planning tools.

73 Games and Activities for the Car

It can be a big job trying to keep kids occupied and out of each other's hair in the car. If constantly pulling over to retrieve dropped toys and screaming, "Stop it!" isn't your thing, try out these kid-tested and mom-approved games and activities for the car.

Toddlers and Preschoolers

Sing-along. Singing in the car is a surefire way to make the time pass quickly. Sing along to CDs or make up words to your own songs.

Surprise! Fill a bag with small wrapped toys and candies. Give one wrapped prize to your child every hour or so. This activity gives kids a great incentive for good behavior. Find inexpensive tokens at your local dollar store that will occupy your kids.

Aluminum foil art. Hand out pieces of aluminum foil to your kids and ask them to create sculptures. They can give their art to their grandparents or friends as "trip gifts," or keep them as prized souvenirs.

I Spy. Think of something that you see in the car and give everyone a clue by saying, "I spy with my little eye something _____," and fill in the blank with a descriptive clue.

Magna Doodle. These magnetic drawing boards make for perfect backseat entertainment. They provide loads of mess-free fun.

My father owns a grocery store. Take turns saying what your father sells by naming items that begin with the letters of the alphabet. "My father owns a grocery store and he sells _____." Fill in the blank with something that begins with the letter *A* and continue, with each person taking a turn, through letter *Z*.

Older Kids

The ABC game. Each person completes the alphabet (in order) by looking for letters on signs and license plates. The person can shout out and point when he or she finds a letter. The first one to get to Z wins.

Black Out Bingo. Give each child a bingo board with pictures of items that you are likely to see. The first one to find and cross off everything on his or her board is the winner.

Catching cars. Name a color and type of car and have your kids try to find it. You may say "green pickup truck" or "yellow two-door car."

License plate game. Have your kids look for license plates from all fifty states. Print out a map and check off the states as you find them.

Spelling bee. Have an old-fashioned spelling bee, asking the children to spell words they've been learning in school. Let your kids ask you to spell words as well.

Magnetic board games. Toy stores sell small travel versions of tic-tac-toe, checkers, and other traditional games that are played on a magnetic board. These games can be great fun for siblings to play in and out of the car.

Handheld games. Handheld games can have their place in the car. Look for inexpensive electronic card games as an alternative to Game Boys and other popular, more expensive options.

The Portable DVD Player

When you're traveling with kids of varying ages to far-away places, the portable DVD player can be a one-size-fits-all source of entertainment. Choose age-appropriate movies or video books and be sure to let your kids know that if they don't behave and aren't quiet, the DVD goes off.

74 Fun Family Traditions

A family tradition is a special event, activity, or observance that children can count on being part of year after year. Family traditions foster a spirit of unity and a sense of belonging. When children don't feel like they're connected to their family, they're likely to look outside their family unit for a connection. Kids may turn to gangs or other undesirable social groups to fulfill their deep desire to belong and to be part of something bigger than themselves.

While we all have family traditions, whether we call them that or not, think about adding to yours by developing a family tradition for each month of the year. Check out this list of ideas to get you started.

January. Adopt a charity to support for the year; take a polar bear plunge; take an annual family photo.

February. Send Valentine's Day cards to nursing home residents; make homemade chocolates.

March. (If Easter falls in March) attend Easter service; color eggs; have an Easter egg hunt; attend an Easter parade.

April. (If Easter falls in April, do the above activities); do spring cleaning; attend a baseball game.

May. Have a Mother's Day dinner; host a Memorial Day cookout; make and deliver homemade cookies to patients of a veteran's hospital.

June. Have an annual family reunion; have a Father's Day dinner.

July. Host a Fourth of July BBQ; watch fireworks; attend a local or state fair.

August. Take a family vacation; go on a weekend camping trip; have backyard Olympics.

September. Go apple picking; visit a farm; have an apple pie bake-off.

October. Host a harvest party; go pumpkin picking; go for a hayride; make a scarecrow.

November. Watch a Thanksgiving Day parade; eat Thanksgiving dinner with another family or relatives; make a list of all the things that you are thankful for.

December. Cut down your own Christmas tree; make a new Christmas ornament; attend Christmas Eve service together; eat Christmas dinner together; donate toys to a charity that helps families in need.

Top Fifteen Family Traditions

According to "The Emergence and Practice of Ritual in the American Family," a report by Jay D. Schvaneveldt and Thomas R. Lee published in *Family Perspective,* the top fifteen family traditions of 1983 were:

1. Christmas
2. birthdays
3. family vacation
4. Easter
5. Sunday dinner
6. visits to relatives
7. fixed time for supper
8. Thanksgiving
9. family reunions
10. family prayer
11. housecleaning routines
12. New Year's Day
13. New Year's Eve
14. father cooking dinner
15. dinner table seating

75 Fifteen Signs of a Family-Friendly Restaurant

Just because a restaurant has a kids' menu doesn't mean that it is family-friendly. Look for these fifteen telltale signs that scream the restaurant's welcome for pint-sized patrons.

A family-friendly restaurant will have:

1. a separately published kids' menu for children under twelve
2. children's menu prices that are about half that of adult selections
3. a few house favorites for children on the kids' menu, in addition to the standards like chicken strips, burgers, and mac-and-cheese
4. beverages and desserts included in the price of the children's meals
5. booths
6. tables without long tablecloths
7. nonglass tabletops
8. bright lighting
9. a place to store strollers
10. easy entrances and exits for strollers
11. high chairs
12. booster seats
13. a diaper-changing station in the bathroom
14. crayons and a placemat or booklet to color, or dough for kids to play with while waiting for their food
15. advertisements in local family publications

Top Twenty-five Family-Friendly Restaurant Chains

Sick of fast-food and take out? Try these family-friendly restaurant chains that warmly welcome little diners.[2]

1. Legal Seafoods
2. Souplantation/Sweet Tomatoes
3. Mimi's Cafe
4. Uno Chicago Grill
5. Chili's Grill and Bar
6. Red Robin
7. Old Spaghetti Factory
8. P. F. Chang's China Bistro

9. Denny's
10. Claim Jumper
11. Cici's Pizza
12. Texas Roadhouse
13. Ted's Montana Grill
14. Joe's Crab Shack
15. California Pizza Kitchen
16. Chevy's Fresh Mex
17. Olive Garden
18. IHOP
19. Roy's
20. Ruby's Diner
21. Bertucci's
22. Sonny's Real Pit BAR-B-Q
23. Applebee's
24. Romano's Macaroni Grill
25. Ruby Tuesday

My Honorable Mentions

Friendly's
Rain Forest Café
Bugaboo Steakhouse

Table Toppers

Disposable, adhesive-backed placemats are a must-have for dining out with babies and toddlers who can't resist picking their plate up off the table. Table Toppers provide a sanitary surface for your children to pick up finger foods from. Check out www.tabletopper.com.

76 The Dos and Don'ts of Dealing with Sibling Rivalry

The sounds of siblings squabbling can be enough to make you want to pull your hair out, but alas, sibling rivalry is a fact of family life. Each child in a family will always vie for his or her parents' attention and strive to be mom's and dad's favorite. To make your home a rivalry-free zone, follow these lists of sibling rivalry dos and don'ts.

When dealing with sibling rivalry, do:

- ✓ *Remember your kids are individuals.* Although they may share some similarities, their personalities and temperaments are wonderfully unique.
- ✓ *Allow for differences.* Encourage the differences that you see in your kids. Foster their distinctive interests and let them know they are loved for who they are.
- ✓ *Let them say, "It's mine."* Allowing children to have things and friends of their own helps them develop as individuals with their own unique personalities. Everyone needs something that they don't have to share.
- ✓ *Encourage alone time.* Facilitate short "sibling free" periods for times of self-discovery.
- ✓ *Spend one-on-one time with each child.* Be proactive in spending alone time with each child. Bath time and reading can be meaningful, short activities that allow you to focus on only one child at a time.
- ✓ *Let them work it out.* Allowing your kids to work out their issues with each other will prevent your taking sides or placing blame when you don't have all the details. If an argument escalates into physical violence, separate

the children; then investigate when things have cooled down.

✓ *Have realistic expectations.* Siblings don't get along all the time. Don't force your kids to play together if they need time apart—we all do!

✓ *Give positive, purposeful praise.* Point out the strengths in each child and praise them when they are interacting well together.

✓ *Have ground rules for behavior.* Have a clear set of rules and expectations for how your children should treat each other. No hitting, no biting, no teasing, and no name-calling should lie at the foundation of your sibling relationship rules. Outlining acceptable and unacceptable behaviors will promote consistency in discipline.

✓ *Spend time together as a family.* This stresses the importance of unity and helps advance a team spirit.

✓ *Develop a system for most wanted privileges.* Having a plan of action in place when it comes to who gets to push the elevator button or who gets to sit on what side of the car will head off heated on-the-spot battles. Keep a coin in the car to toss or keep track of who did what last to settle disputes over the most coveted privileges.

✓ *Let your kids express their feelings.* Encourage your children to communicate their feelings. Helping your kids find the words to express their emotions gives them a sense of control. Be sure to validate feelings without validating negative behavior. "I know you are frustrated, but hands aren't for hitting" empowers the child without condoning the behavior.

✓ *Model good behavior.* You reap what you sow when it comes to childhood behaviors. Model positive interactions with your spouse and your kids and you'll be surprised at how quickly it gets mirrored back.

✓ *Be fair.* Hold all your children accountable for the same rules and regulations and follow through on the same consequences for any misbehavior.

When dealing with sibling rivalry, don't:

Ø *Don't compare your kids.* Recognize that comparing your kids sets the stage for their comparing themselves with each other. These seemingly innocent comparisons are at the root of sibling rivalry.

Ø *Don't use competition to motivate.* Recognize the heightened sense of natural competition that already exists among siblings and don't add to it. Have them race against a timer rather than each other when picking up toys.

Ø *Don't try to always treat them the same.* If you treat your kids differently, it's okay! They *are* different. Meeting each child's unique needs is what is important. Just because Sean wore his shoes out and got a new pair doesn't mean Jane has to if hers are perfectly fine.

Ø *Don't be concerned with who started a fight.* It takes two to quarrel. Hold your kids accountable for their actions.

Ø *Don't label.* Be careful not to mold your kids with your words. Labels can last a lifetime, and your kids will either live up to or down to your expectations.

Ø *Don't take sides.* Be an impartial mediator and resist the urge to figure out who did what—it's nearly impossible to figure out the blow-by-blow when you just catch the end of the match.

77 Five Steps for Fostering Friendships

During the preschool years, nearly everyone a child meets becomes his friend, but around age five or six, kids really begin to understand the reciprocal bond that friends share. During the early years, friendships provide important opportunities for children to experience acceptance, learn how to trust, practice their social skills, and engage a variety of different personalities.

To help your child build friendships:

1. *Provide opportunities for your child to interact with his peers.* Play groups, Sunday school class, and playtime at the local playground can provide great opportunities for your child to connect with his peers. See List 57 for tips on hosting a successful playdate.
2. *Enroll your child in programs that he has an interest in.* When your child is in a class that interests him, he's likely to meet others who share the same interest. Weekly story time at the local library is a no-cost activity that most young children love.
3. *Teach your child to introduce himself.* Increase your child's self-confidence by giving him the tools he needs to engage other kids. Role-play introductory conversations and let him practice introducing himself to others. Encourage your child to smile and greet others when entering a room.
4. *Encourage your child to share.* A child who is easy to play with and who will take turns is a playmate that everyone will want to have.

5. *Teach your child to handle defeat gracefully.* From losing a game to being rejected by a potential friend, every child will have his moments of defeat. Teach your child good sportsmanship and acknowledge your child's hurt feelings without validating socially unacceptable behaviors.

The Golden Rules of Friendship to Teach Your Kids

Be kind. Be nice; don't tease, name call, or intentionally hurt your friend's feelings.

Be honest. Always tell the truth; don't lie to your friends.

Be loyal. Be a friend all of the time; don't be a fair-weather friend.

Be respectful. Treat your friend like a valued person; don't take your friend for granted.

Be fair. Compromise with your friend and take turns; be sure to give as much as you take; don't make your friend always do what you want to do.

Be supportive. Listen to what your friend has to say; encourage, don't discourage, your friend.

78 United States Federal Holidays

It can be hard to keep track of the holidays for which schools close and those on which they stay open. On federal holidays, all nonessential federal offices, including banks and public schools, are closed. Most private banks and private schools also close on federal holidays.

There are ten U.S. federal holidays.[3]

New Year's Day—January 1
Martin Luther King's Birthday—third Monday in January
Washington's Birthday—third Monday in February
Memorial Day—last Monday in May
Independence Day—July 4
Labor Day—first Monday in September
Columbus Day—second Monday in October
Veteran's Day—November 11
Thanksgiving Day—fourth Thursday in November
Christmas Day—December 25

79 Bible Basics

When talking to your child about the Bible, you may be wondering where to start. Introduce your children to these basic Bible teachings.

The Ten Commandments

Exodus 20:1–17

And God spoke all these words, saying: "I am the LORD your God."

Exodus 20:1 NKJV

	Adult Version	Kids Version[4]
1	You shall have no other gods before Me.	Love God the most.
2	You shall not make for yourself a carved image—any likeness of anything that is in heaven above, or that is in the earth beneath, or that is in the water under the earth.	Put God first.
3	You shall not take the name of the LORD your God in vain.	Always use God's name respectfully.
4	Remember the Sabbath day, to keep it holy.	Honor the Lord by resting on Sunday.
5	Honor your father and your mother.	Love and obey your parents.
6	You shall not murder.	Do not hurt people.
7	You shall not commit adultery.	Be faithful to your husband or wife.
8	You shall not steal.	Don't take things that don't belong to you.
9	You shall not bear false witness against your neighbor.	Always tell the truth.
10	You shall not covet your neighbor's house; you shall not covet your neighbor's wife, nor his male servant, nor his female servant, nor his ox, nor his donkey, nor anything that is your neighbor's.	Be happy with the things you have and don't wish to have the things other people have.

The Greatest Commandment

"Teacher, which is the greatest commandment in the Law?"

Jesus replied: "'Love the Lord your God with all your heart and with all your soul and with all your mind.' This is the first and greatest commandment. And the second is like it: 'Love your neighbor as yourself.' All the Law and the Prophets hang on these two commandments."

Matthew 22:36–40

How can you get this message across to young hearts? Write each of the Ten Commandments on a strip of paper and have your child arrange them in the order she thinks is most important. Then arrange them in the order in which they are written. Take time to point out that the first four commandments talk about loving God, while the last six talk about loving others. This is a great visual activity to show why God tells us that love is the greatest commandment of all.

The Golden Rule

So in everything, do to others what you would have them do to you.

Matthew 7:12

In kidspeak: Treat others the way you want them to treat you.

ABCs of Salvation

Admit that you have sinned.

"All have sinned and fall short of the glory of God" (Rom. 3:23).

"If we say that we have no sin, we deceive ourselves, and the truth is not in us" (1 John 1:8 NKJV).

Believe in Jesus.

"For God so loved the world that he gave his one and only Son, that whoever believes in him shall not perish but have eternal life" (John 3:16).

"Believe on the Lord Jesus Christ, and you will be saved" (Acts 16:31 NKJV).

Confess and turn from your sin.

"If you confess with your mouth the Lord Jesus and believe in your heart that God has raised Him from the dead, you will be saved" (Rom. 10:9 NKJV).

"Whoever calls on the name of the LORD shall be saved" (Rom. 10:13 NKJV).

In Kidspeak:

Admit it! All of us are bad, including me.

Believe it! Believe God loves you and sent Jesus to save you from your sins.

Confess it! Commit yourself to follow Jesus.

80 Thirty Ways to Document Your Family's Heritage and Favorite Memories

At one point or another, every child has a deep desire to know where he came from. He'll ask questions ranging from "What was it like when you were growing up?" to "How did Nana and Papa meet?" Documenting your family history and recording your favorite family memories can help you answer your child's questions and give him the information he'll need to someday answer the questions that his children will ask him.

1. Save a newspaper from the day your child was born.
2. Keep a baby book for each child.
3. Fill up photo albums with family photos to pass on to your children.
4. Make a family scrapbook.
5. Create digital slide shows and save them to CDs and DVDs.
6. Take video footage for an annual family movie.

7. Record interviews with family members.
8. Fill in your family tree.
9. Take an annual family photo.
10. Compile cherished family recipes.
11. Use a fill-in-the-blank memory book for your children.
12. Keep a journal.
13. Pass on a family hobby. For example: if you knit, teach your daughter to knit.
14. Save letters you've received.
15. Carry on with family traditions from your childhood.
16. Write down what you know about past generations of your family.
17. Make a time capsule the year your child was born.
18. Make a photo patchwork quilt.
19. Tell favorite family stories often.
20. Collect documents and official records of family members.
21. Ask older family members to write letters to your children.
22. Have old family movies transferred to newer formats.
23. Collect postcards from your travels.
24. Inscribe your favorite book to pass down from generation to generation.
25. Pass down a family Bible.
26. Write a book about your family.
27. Display family heirlooms and create a photo journal of them. Include any history behind them, such as who they belonged to or how they were obtained.
28. Maintain a family website.
29. Encourage your children to keep a diary.
30. Pass down a favorite piece of jewelry to a child, explaining its significance.

I thank my God every time I remember you.

Philippians 1:3

Tips for Preserving Your Family Photos

1. Develop or print your photos immediately after taking them. Order one set of prints for yourself and one for each of your children.
2. File your pictures chronologically in a shoe or photo storage box until you're ready to do something more with them.
3. Purchase an archival-quality photo album for yourself and each of your children and fill it chronologically with photos.
4. Make one high-quality family scrapbook or photo album. Label people and places in your photos and include any other key information in your album.
5. If you're using digital photography, store copies of your photos on disk. You can also upload photos to an Internet album, using a free storage service like the ones provided by Snapfish (www.snapfish .com) or Shutterfly (www.shutterfly.com). Consider using one of these services to print an annual family photo album.

81 A Dozen Tips for Teaching Acceptance of All without Compromising Your Family Values and Beliefs

Kids aren't born with an understanding of God's truth; they need to be taught it. In today's world, kids will be exposed to everything from the theory of evolution to homosexuality. They'll learn about worldly things from friends, from school, and from the media. Christian parents need to equip their children to handle these confrontations in a head-on, godly way. Teach your child to accept all people without compromising your family values, using these twelve tips.

1. *Teach your kids the whole gospel.* When children are young, emphasize the love of God and relate it to how a mom or a dad loves his or her child. "We all do bad things, right? But just as Mom and Dad never stop loving you, God doesn't stop either. Mom and Dad will guide you to a better way to do things, and God will do the same—the way a shepherd steers his sheep away from harmful things toward good things."

2. *Be a loving example, and your kids will learn to be loving too.* With young kids, it is important to use the power of your example more than the example of your power. We need to show people how Jesus loves us. When we see someone who needs help, we should help him or her. When we see someone who is sad, we should try to cheer up that person.

3. *Teach your kids to accept everyone, but not every belief.* Say to your children, "You're going to hear that people believe different things about God than we do. But when we wonder if what we're hearing is true, we can go back and look in God's Word to be sure."

4. *Separate the essentials from the nonessentials.* Teach your child that, while some things can keep you from a relationship with God, in other things there is room for disagreement (see 2 Tim. 2:23; Titus 3:9). Some people pray differently or go to churches that sing different songs, but as long as they believe in Jesus, they are part of the family of God. And even if they don't believe in Jesus, God loves them, and we need to love them too.

5. *Be biblical judges.* Don't judge for yourself what is acceptable and unacceptable; instead, compare everything to the Bible. Teach your kids to look to the Bible, not to popular opinion or to the media, for their standard of living. When we don't know if something is okay, we can look to see what God tells us in the Bible.
6. *Have family rules.* Set a standard of living for your family based on the Bible. Communicate why you choose to live the way you do. You can say to your children: "We don't do that because we don't believe it's okay with God."
7. *Make judgment calls for your own kids, not for their friends.* Use the phrase: "It's just not something we do in our family," rather than, "They're bad parents because they let their kids do that."
8. *Teach kids to disagree without being degrading.* We are called to be full of grace and truth (see John 1:14).
9. *Build positive peer pressure.* Get your kids involved with other Christian kids. They'll offer the peer support that they need to meet confrontations head-on and with the right attitude. Give this advice to your children: "Make friends with the kids in church. It's great to have friends who believe what you do."
10. *Be a role model.* Say what you want your kids to say, and do what you want your kids to do.
11. *Teach empathy.* Ask your children, "Would you feel that God loved you if he said, 'You can't play with us because you say bad words'? When you see someone who has no one to play with, invite her to play along with you."
12. *Encourage your kids to evangelize.* Everyone is worthy of hearing the Good News. Role-play how to share the gospel with kids who have different beliefs and lifestyles than you. Your children can tell others: "Jesus loves you."

Pursuing truth in this context means countering the new doctrine of tolerance. It means teaching our children to embrace all people, but not all beliefs. It means showing them how to listen to and learn from all people without necessarily agreeing with them. It means helping them courageously but humbly speak the truth, even if it makes them the object of scorn or hatred.

Josh McDowell[5]

Tolerance vs. Love

Tolerance says, "You must approve of what I do."

Love responds, "I must do something harder; I will love you, even when your behavior offends me."

Tolerance says, "You must agree with me."

Love responds, "I must do something harder; I will tell you the truth, because I am convinced 'the truth will set you free.'"

Tolerance says, "You must allow me to have my way."

Love responds, "I must do something harder; I will plead with you to follow the right way, because I believe you are worth the risk."

Tolerance seeks to be inoffensive; love takes risks.

Tolerance glorifies division; love seeks unity.

Tolerance costs nothing; love costs everything.[6]

LISTS FOR GENERAL HEALTH AND SAFETY

82 Common Childhood Allergies

Ten to 20 percent of all children suffer from allergies. In infants and in young children, allergies often present themselves as skin rashes. Many infants and young children suffer from eczema. Eczema is the rash associated with atopic dermatitis. Atopic dermatitis is a chronic disease that presents itself as an itch that, when scratched, creates a dry and red skin rash on the face, scalp, chest, trunk, and limbs of young children. This rash is known as eczema.[1] The itch is usually caused by an allergic reaction to an irritant that has come in contact with the skin, an infection, or a food. Avoiding triggers that cause itching can help to prevent eczema.

Food allergy symptoms can include vomiting, diarrhea, difficulty breathing, and a runny nose, in addition to a skin rash.[2] Usually these symptoms occur within a short time from when the food allergen is ingested. Keeping a dietary journal that notes your child's reaction to foods can help to pinpoint a food allergy. If your child has a food allergy, it is important, of course, to avoid that food. Carefully read all food labels to keep foods that have the allergen as an ingredient from your child.

Top Seven Food Allergens[3]

eggs	soy
milk	wheat

peanuts   seafood
tree nuts

Common Allergens in the Home

mold   chemicals
dust mites   cleaners
animal dander   cosmetics
medications   perfumes

Common Outdoor Allergens

trees   weeds
grass   pollen

Allergy Symptoms

In older children allergies may present themselves in a variety of ways. Some common symptoms that may indicate a possible allergy include:

congestion   skin rash
runny nose   swelling
sneezing   diarrhea
watery eyes   vomiting
eczema   asthma
hives   hay fever
itchy nose, eyes, and
    mouth

Food Allergy versus Food Intolerance

Food intolerances are often confused for food allergies. True food allergies involve the immune system, while food intolerances are a result of the body's inability to digest certain foods.

Anaphylaxis Shock

Although anaphylaxis shock is rare, it is an extreme allergic reaction and requires immediate medical attention. Symptoms of anaphylaxis shock may include difficulty breathing; swelling of the face, lips, throat, and tongue; a drop in blood pressure; and a sense of tightening of the throat.

Allergy Facts

If one parent has allergies, a child has a 40 percent chance of having allergies. If both parents have allergies the chance that their child will have allergies goes up to 80 percent.[4]

Skin tests and blood tests can be used to identify allergens. Speak to your child's pediatrician about seeing an allergist if you suspect that your child is suffering from allergies.

Breastfeeding exclusively for the first 6 months can prevent the onset of allergies.

██LIST██ 83 Common Childhood Illnesses That Involve Rashes

While the following illnesses don't usually warrant an emergency visit to the doctor, it's always a good idea to confirm your diagnostic suspicions with your child's health-care provider as soon as possible.

Rash	Symptoms	Cause	Treatment	Bearing Contagion
Hives[5]	welts on the body that come and go	allergic reaction, virus, or cold	For children over one year of age, give Benadryl; avoid allergens.	no
Eczema[6]	flat and dry patches or red, raised patches during flare-ups	dry skin or allergies	Use 1 percent hydrocortisone cream; avoid allergens.	no
Chicken pox[7]	red spots that turn to blisters, which crust over; fever	virus	For children over one year of age, give Benadryl; oatmeal baths can provide relief; give nonaspirin pain reliever for high fevers.	yes, on day before fever or rash appears until twenty-four hours after all spots have crusted over
Fifth's disease[8]	appearance of slapped cheeks; lacy pimple-type rash on trunk, spreading to arms and legs	virus	Treat bothersome symptoms.	yes, on day before rash and fever appear until twenty-four hours after fever breaks on its own

Rash	Symptoms	Cause	Treatment	Bearing Contagion
Roseola[9]	fever followed by a rash, consisting of red spots and bumps, spreading from the neck and back down to trunk and arms and legs	virus	Treat bothersome symptoms.	yes, on day before rash and fever appear until twenty-four hours after fever breaks on its own
Coxsackie[10]	blisters on hands, feet, and mouth— also known as hand, foot, and mouth disease	virus	Give cold drinks, Benadryl, and pain reliever.	yes, until fever has been gone for two days
Heat rash[11]	tiny pimples or spots on neck or back	heat, sweat, and clothing rubbing against the body	Cool off child; apply a cool cloth to affected area.	no
Impetigo[12]	raised bumps with honey-colored crust usually on face and around mouth	bacterial infection	Mild cases: clean area with soapy water and apply diluted hydrogen peroxide and topical antibiotic ointment. Severe cases: ask the doctor for a prescription.	yes, by direct contact with skin eruptions
Ringworm[13]	ring-shaped rash with borders, has scales, blisters, or bumps	fungus infection	Apply a topical antifungal cream.	yes, by direct contact with lesions

Rash	Symptoms	Cause	Treatment	Bearing Contagion
Warts[14]	skin-colored bumps	virus	For home treatment: use over the counter salicylic acid wart remover or place duct tape over the wart for one week, soak area in water and remove tape, then rub wart with emery board. Repeat process until wart is gone. A doctor can freeze warts off or apply stronger acids.	the virus that causes warts is contagious, but the warts themselves are not

When Should You Make an Urgent Call to the Doctor?

If your infant has any type of rash, you should immediately contact your child's health-care provider.

If you notice tiny pinpoint, red, flat dots on your child's body that do not turn white when you press on them, call your child's doctor immediately. This could be petechiae or purpura, caused by broken blood vessels underneath the skin and could be a sign of bleeding or serious infection.[15]

84 Standard Vaccination Schedule for Children

The purpose of vaccinations is to immunize children against disease. Vaccinations contain mild versions of the same germs present in diseases. When children are injected with these weakened strains of disease, their bodies create antibodies that destroy the germs. Following a vaccination, the antibodies stay in your child's system and will protect him if he is exposed to the disease against which he was vaccinated. Today children in the United States are routinely vaccinated against fourteen diseases.[16]

Fourteen Diseases Children Are Routinely Vaccinated Against

1. diphtheria
2. hepatitis A
3. hepatitis B
4. Hib disease
5. influenza (flu)
6. measles
7. mumps
8. pertussis (whooping cough)
9. pneumococcal disease
10. polio
11. rotavirus
12. rubella (German measles)
13. tetanus
14. varicella (chicken pox)

Before Vaccinating Your Child

- Speak to your child's heath-care provider about why your child should be vaccinated and about any vaccination concerns that you may have.
- Do your research. Know what vaccinations your child is scheduled to receive and their possible side effects.
- Know how many shots your child will get. Some practitioners combine vaccinations to minimize the number of sticks.
- Know what to do if your child does experience an adverse reaction to a vaccination he received.
- Know your school or child care provider's policy on vaccinations.
- Ask your pediatrician if he or she recommends routinely giving pain medication right before or immediately following vaccinations.

Do Vaccines Cause Autism?

According to the Center for Disease Control, vaccines do not cause autism: "The weight of currently available scientific evidence does not support the hypothesis that vaccines cause autism."[17]

Do Vaccinations Really Contain Human Fetal Cells?

Two different strains of human diploid cell cultures made from aborted fetuses have been used for vaccine production since the 1960s. One was developed in the United States in 1961 (called WI-38) and the other in the United Kingdom in 1966 (called MRC-5). Common vaccines that contain these cells include Rubella, Hep A, Chicken Pox, and Rabies.

The viruses cannot reproduce on their own so they must be grown in a biological host. These self-reproducing cells serve as the host for the viruses to grow. Because these cells continue to reproduce on their own, there is no need for additional abortions to produce vaccinations.[18]

Even within the Christian community, parents and doctors are divided about vaccinating their children using a cell line derived from aborted fetuses. It's important to remember that the decision to vaccinate your child is a decision of conscience and not one of salvation. Whether you vaccinate your child or not will not impact your place in eternity.

While using vaccinations made from a non-fetal cell line is ideal, currently this alternative is not available in the United States for most vaccinations that currently use the fetal cell lines.

Because of the widespread use of vaccinations, infectous diseases have been controlled and often eliminated, resulting in countless lives saved.

The Christian Medical & Dental Associations (www.CMDA.org) is a great resource for parents seeking more information about vaccinations. I have found their board members most helpful and willing to personally respond to inquiries from parents.

Recommended Immunization Schedule for Persons Aged 0 Through 6 Years—United States • 2009

For those who fall behind or start late, see the catch-up schedule

Vaccine ▼ Age ▶	Birth	1 month	2 months	4 months	6 months	12 months	15 months	18 months	19–23 months	2–3 years	4–6 years
Hepatitis B[1]	HepB	HepB		see footnote 1	HepB						
Rotavirus[2]			RV	RV	RV[2]						
Diphtheria, Tetanus, Pertussis[3]			DTaP	DTaP	DTaP	see footnote3	DTaP	DTaP			DTaP
Haemophilus influenzae type b[4]			Hib	Hib	Hib[4]	Hib	Hib				
Pneumococcal[5]			PCV	PCV	PCV	PCV	PCV			PPSV	PPSV
Inactivated Poliovirus			IPV	IPV	IPV	IPV	IPV	IPV			IPV
Influenza[6]						Influenza (Yearly)					
Measles, Mumps, Rubella[7]						MMR	MMR		see footnote 7		MMR
Varicella[8]						Varicella	Varicella		see footnote 8		Varicella
Hepatitis A[9]						HepA (2 doses)	HepA (2 doses)	HepA (2 doses)	HepA (2 doses)	HepA Series	HepA Series
Meningococcal[10]										MCV	MCV

Range of recommended ages

Certain high-risk groups

This schedule indicates the recommended ages for routine administration of currently licensed vaccines, as of December 1, 2008, for children aged 0 through 6 years. Any dose not administered at the recommended age should be administered at a subsequent visit, when indicated and feasible. Licensed combination vaccines may be used whenever any component of the combination is indicated and other components are not contraindicated and if approved by the Food and Drug Administration for that dose of the series. Providers should consult the relevant Advisory Committee on Immunization Practices statement for detailed recommendations, including high-risk conditions: http://www.cdc.gov/vaccines/pubs/acip-list.htm. Clinically significant adverse events that follow immunization should be reported to the Vaccine Adverse Event Reporting System (VAERS). Guidance about how to obtain and complete a VAERS form is available at http://www.vaers.hhs.gov or by telephone, 800-822-7967.

1. Hepatitis B vaccine (HepB). *(Minimum age: birth)*

At birth:

- Administer monovalent HepB to all newborns before hospital discharge.
- If mother is hepatitis B surface antigen (HBsAg)-positive, administer HepB and 0.5 mL of hepatitis B immune globulin (HBIG) within 12 hours of birth.
- If mother's HBsAg status is unknown, administer HepB within 12 hours of birth. Determine mother's HBsAg status as soon as possible and, if HBsAg-positive, administer HBIG (no later than age 1 week).

After the birth dose:

- The HepB series should be completed with either monovalent HepB or a combination vaccine containing HepB. The second dose should be administered at age 1 or 2 months. The final dose should be administered no earlier than age 24 weeks.
- Infants born to HBsAg-positive mothers should be tested for HBsAg and antibody to HBsAg (anti-HBs) after completion of at least 3 doses of the HepB series, at age 9 through 18 months (generally at the next well-child visit).

4-month dose:

- Administration of 4 doses of HepB to infants is permissible when combination vaccines containing HepB are administered after the birth dose.

2. Rotavirus vaccine (RV). *(Minimum age: 6 weeks)*

- Administer the first dose at age 6 through 14 weeks (maximum age: 14 weeks 6 days). Vaccination should not be initiated for infants aged 15 weeks or older (i.e., 15 weeks 0 days or older).
- Administer the final dose in the series by age 8 months 0 days.
- If Rotarix® is administered at ages 2 and 4 months, a dose at 6 months is not indicated.

3. Diphtheria and tetanus toxoids and acellular pertussis vaccine (DTaP). *(Minimum age: 6 weeks)*

- The fourth dose may be administered as early as age 12 months, provided at least 6 months have elapsed since the third dose.
- Administer the final dose in the series at age 4 through 6 years.

4. Haemophilus influenzae type b conjugate vaccine (Hib). *(Minimum age: 6 weeks)*

- If PRP-OMP (PedvaxHIB® or Comvax® [HepB-Hib]) is administered at ages 2 and 4 months, a dose at age 6 months is not indicated.
- TriHiBit® (DTaP/Hib) should not be used for doses at ages 2, 4, or 6 months but can be used as the final dose in children aged 12 months or older.

5. Pneumococcal vaccine. *(Minimum age: 6 weeks for pneumococcal conjugate vaccine [PCV]; 2 years for pneumococcal polysaccharide vaccine [PPSV])*

- PCV is recommended for all children aged younger than 5 years. Administer 1 dose of PCV to all healthy children aged 24 through 59 months who are not completely vaccinated for their age.

- Administer PPSV to children aged 2 years or older with certain underlying medical conditions (see *MMWR* 2000;49[No. RR-9]), including a cochlear implant.

6. Influenza vaccine. *(Minimum age: 6 months for trivalent inactivated influenza vaccine [TIV]; 2 years for live, attenuated influenza vaccine [LAIV])*

- Administer annually to children aged 6 months through 18 years.
- For healthy nonpregnant persons (i.e., those who do not have underlying medical conditions that predispose them to influenza complications) aged 2 through 49 years, either LAIV or TIV may be used.
- Children receiving TIV should receive 0.25 mL if aged 6 through 35 months or 0.5 mL if aged 3 years or older.
- Administer 2 doses (separated by at least 4 weeks) to children aged younger than 9 years who are receiving influenza vaccine for the first time or who were vaccinated for the first time during the previous influenza season but only received 1 dose.

7. Measles, mumps, and rubella vaccine (MMR). *(Minimum age: 12 months)*

- Administer the second dose at age 4 through 6 years. However, the second dose may be administered before age 4, provided at least 28 days have elapsed since the first dose.

8. Varicella vaccine. *(Minimum age: 12 months)*

- Administer the second dose at age 4 through 6 years. However, the second dose may be administered before age 4, provided at least 3 months have elapsed since the first dose.
- For children aged 12 months through 12 years the minimum interval between doses is 3 months. However, if the second dose was administered at least 28 days after the first dose, it can be accepted as valid.

9. Hepatitis A vaccine (HepA). *(Minimum age: 12 months)*

- Administer to all children aged 1 year (i.e., aged 12 through 23 months). Administer 2 doses at least 6 months apart.
- Children not fully vaccinated by age 2 years can be vaccinated at subsequent visits.
- HepA also is recommended for children older than 1 year who live in areas where vaccination programs target older children or who are at increased risk of infection. See *MMWR* 2006;55(No. RR-7).

10. Meningococcal vaccine. *(Minimum age: 2 years for meningococcal conjugate vaccine [MCV] and for meningococcal polysaccharide vaccine [MPSV])*

- Administer MCV to children aged 2 through 10 years with terminal complement component deficiency, anatomic or functional asplenia, and certain other high-risk groups. See *MMWR* 2005;54(No. RR-7).
- Persons who received MPSV 3 or more years previously and who remain at increased risk for meningococcal disease should be revaccinated with MCV.

The Recommended Immunization Schedules for Persons Aged 0 Through 18 Years are approved by the Advisory Committee on Immunization Practices (www.cdc.gov/vaccines/recs/acip), the American Academy of Pediatrics (http://www.aap.org), and the American Academy of Family Physicians (http://www.aafp.org).

DEPARTMENT OF HEALTH AND HUMAN SERVICES • CENTERS FOR DISEASE CONTROL AND PREVENTION

Catch-up Immunization Schedule for Persons Aged 4 Months Through 18 Years Who Start Late or Who Are More Than 1 Month Behind—United States • 2009

The table below provides catch-up schedules and minimum intervals between doses for children whose vaccinations have been delayed. A vaccine series does not need to be restarted, regardless of the time that has elapsed between doses. Use the section appropriate for the child's age.

CATCH-UP SCHEDULE FOR PERSONS AGED 4 MONTHS THROUGH 6 YEARS

Vaccine	Minimum Age for Dose 1	Dose 1 to Dose 2	Dose 2 to Dose 3	Dose 3 to Dose 4	Dose 4 to Dose 5
			Minimum Interval Between Doses		
Hepatitis B[1]	Birth	4 weeks	8 weeks (and at least 16 weeks after first dose)		
Rotavirus[2]	6 wks	4 weeks	4 weeks[2]		
Diphtheria, Tetanus, Pertussis[3]	6 wks	4 weeks	4 weeks	6 months	6 months[3]
Haemophilus influenzae type b[4]	6 wks	**4 weeks** if first dose administered at younger than age 12 months **8 weeks (as final dose)** if first dose administered at age 12-14 months **No further doses needed** if first dose administered at age 15 months or older	**4 weeks**[4] if current age is younger than 12 months **8 weeks (as final dose)**[4] if current age is 12 months or older and second dose administered at younger than age 15 months **No further doses needed** if previous dose administered at age 15 months or older	**8 weeks (as final dose)** This dose only necessary for children aged 12 months through 59 months who received 3 doses before age 12 months	
Pneumococcal[5]	6 wks	**4 weeks** if first dose administered at younger than age 12 months **8 weeks (as final dose for healthy children)** if first dose administered at age 12 months or older or current age 24 through 59 months **No further doses needed** for healthy children if first dose administered at age 24 months or older	**4 weeks** if current age is younger than 12 months **8 weeks** (as final dose for healthy children) if current age is 12 months or older **No further doses needed** for healthy children if previous dose administered at age 24 months or older	**8 weeks (as final dose)** This dose only necessary for children aged 12 months through 59 months who received 3 doses before age 12 months or for high-risk children who received 3 doses at any age	
Inactivated Poliovirus[6]	6 wks	4 weeks	4 weeks	4 weeks[6]	
Measles, Mumps, Rubella[7]	12 mos	4 weeks			
Varicella[8]	12 mos	3 months			
Hepatitis A[9]	12 mos	6 months			

CATCH-UP SCHEDULE FOR PERSONS AGED 7 THROUGH 18 YEARS

Vaccine	Minimum Age for Dose 1	Dose 1 to Dose 2	Dose 2 to Dose 3	Dose 3 to Dose 4	Dose 4 to Dose 5
Tetanus, Diphtheria/ Tetanus, Diphtheria, Pertussis[10]	7 yrs[10]	4 weeks	**4 weeks** if first dose administered at younger than age 12 months **6 months** if first dose administered at age 12 months or older	**6 months** if first dose administered at younger than age 12 months	

Routine dosing intervals are recommended[11]

Vaccine	Minimum Age for Dose 1	Dose 1 to Dose 2	Dose 2 to Dose 3	Dose 3 to Dose 4
Human Papillomavirus[11]	9 yrs			
Hepatitis A[9]	12 mos	6 months		
Hepatitis B[1]	Birth	4 weeks	8 weeks (and at least 16 weeks after first dose)	
Inactivated Poliovirus[6]	6 wks	4 weeks	4 weeks	4 weeks[6]
Measles, Mumps, Rubella[7]	12 mos	4 weeks		
Varicella[8]	12 mos	3 months if the person is younger than age 13 years; 4 weeks if the person is aged 13 years or older		

1. Hepatitis B vaccine (HepB).
• Administer the 3-dose series to those not previously vaccinated.
• A 2-dose series (separated by at least 4 months) of adult formulation Recombivax HB® is licensed for children aged 11 through 15 years.

2. Rotavirus vaccine (RV).
• The maximum age for the first dose is 14 weeks 6 days. Vaccination should not be initiated for infants aged 15 weeks or older (i.e., 15 weeks 0 days).
• Administer the final dose in the series by age 8 months 0 days.
• If Rotarix® was administered for the first and second doses, a third dose is not indicated.

3. Diphtheria and tetanus toxoids and acellular pertussis vaccine (DTaP).
• The fifth dose is not necessary if the fourth dose was administered at age 4 years or older.

4. Haemophilus influenzae type b conjugate vaccine (Hib).
• Hib vaccine is not generally recommended for persons aged 5 years or older. No efficacy data are available on which to base a recommendation concerning use of Hib vaccine for older children and adults. However, studies suggest good immunogenicity in persons who have sickle cell disease, leukemia, or HIV infection, or who have had a splenectomy; administering 1 dose of Hib vaccine to these persons is not contraindicated.
• If the first 2 doses were PRP-OMP (PedvaxHIB® or Comvax®), and administered at age 11 months or younger, the third (and final) dose should be administered at age 12 through 15 months and at least 8 weeks after the second dose.
• If the first dose was administered at age 7 through 11 months, administer 2 doses separated by 4 weeks and a final dose at age 12 through 15 months.

5. Pneumococcal vaccine.
• Administer 1 dose of pneumococcal conjugate vaccine (PCV) to all healthy children aged 24 through 59 months who have not received at least 1 dose of PCV on or after age 12 months.
• For children aged 24 through 59 months with underlying medical conditions, administer 1 dose of PCV if 3 doses were received previously or administer 2 doses of PCV at least 8 weeks apart if fewer than 3 doses were received previously.
• Administer pneumococcal polysaccharide vaccine (PPSV) to children aged 2 years or older with certain underlying medical conditions (see MMWR 2000;49[No. RR-9]), including a cochlear implant, at least 8 weeks after the last dose of PCV.

6. Inactivated poliovirus vaccine (IPV).
• For children who received an all-IPV or all-oral poliovirus (OPV) series, a fourth dose is not necessary if the third dose was administered at age 4 years or older.
• If both OPV and IPV were administered as part of a series, a total of 4 doses should be administered, regardless of the child's current age.

7. Measles, mumps, and rubella vaccine (MMR).
• Administer the second dose at age 4 through 6 years. However, the second dose may be administered before age 4, provided at least 28 days have elapsed since the first dose.
• If not previously vaccinated, administer 2 doses with at least 28 days between doses.

8. Varicella vaccine.
• Administer the second dose at age 4 through 6 years. However, the second dose may be administered before age 4, provided at least 3 months have elapsed since the first dose.
• For persons aged 12 months through 12 years, the minimum interval between doses is 3 months. However, if the second dose was administered at least 28 days after the first dose, it can be accepted as valid.
• For persons aged 13 years and older, the minimum interval between doses is 28 days.

9. Hepatitis A vaccine (HepA).
• HepA is recommended for children older than 1 year who live in areas where vaccination programs target older children or who are at increased risk of infection. See MMWR 2006;55(No. RR-7).

10. Tetanus and diphtheria toxoids vaccine (Td) and tetanus and diphtheria toxoids and acellular pertussis vaccine (Tdap).
• Doses of DTaP are counted as part of the Td/Tdap series
• Tdap should be substituted for a single dose of Td in the catch-up series or as a booster for children aged 10 through 18 years; use Td for other doses.

11. Human papillomavirus vaccine (HPV).
• Administer the series to females at age 13 through 18 years if not previously vaccinated.
• Use recommended routine dosing intervals for series catch-up (i.e., the second and third doses should be administered at 2 and 6 months after the first dose). However, the minimum interval between the first and second doses is 4 weeks. The minimum interval between the second and third doses is 12 weeks, and the third dose should be given at least 24 weeks after the first dose.

Information about reporting reactions after immunization is available online at http://www.vaers.hhs.gov or by telephone, 800-822-7967. Suspected cases of vaccine-preventable diseases should be reported to the state or local health department. Additional information, including precautions and contraindications for immunization, is available from the National Center for Immunization and Respiratory Diseases at http://www.cdc.gov/vaccines or telephone, 800-CDC-INFO (800-232-4636).

DEPARTMENT OF HEALTH AND HUMAN SERVICES • CENTERS FOR DISEASE CONTROL AND PREVENTION

85 When to Call the Doctor

Many parents wonder when they should call the doctor. You should always call the doctor if your child is lethargic, unresponsive, and refusing to eat; has an unidentifiable rash; is having difficulty breathing; or has a fever lasting more than a few days. Most pediatricians' offices have a "nurse's line" that parents can call to get medical advice. Take advantage of this helpful resource.

Ten Symptoms You Shouldn't Ignore

1. A temperature in a young baby. If your baby is younger than 2 to 4 months and has a fever (over 99.4 orally or 100.4 rectally), call the pediatrician immediately.
2. A prolonged temperature in an older child. A child with a fever for more than 72 hours or a child who has a fever and is fussy or lethargic should be evaluated by the doctor.
3. Dehydration due to vomiting and/or diarrhea.
4. Persistent vomiting or any vomiting with blood or bile or vomiting that is green or projectile.
5. Bloody stool.
6. A lethargic child, a confused child, a child who seems excessively sleepy, or a child who just doesn't seem right.
7. Difficult or noisy breathing.
8. A child who complains of a bellyache.
9. Limping or any other indication of an injury.
10. Significant swelling or bruising.

Croup

Coughing that sounds like a seal bark could indicate a viral illness called croup. To treat croup, take your child outdoors to breathe cold air or into a steamy bathroom to breathe moist, warm air. If this does not help, call your doctor.

86 Basic First Aid for Ten Common Childhood Injuries

Not every injury requires an immediate trip to the doctor. In fact many minor injuries can often be treated at home. Use the following prescribed first aid treatments for common childhood injuries, and always follow up treatment with a call to your child's doctor.

1. *Minor animal bite wounds.* Wash the affected area with soap and water and apply antibiotic ointment to prevent infection. Cover with a clean adhesive bandage. Call your doctor or seek emergency medical care.
2. *Minor burns.* Cool the burn by running cold water over the affected area or by immersing the affected area in cold water for several minutes. Do not use ice. Cover the burn area loosely with sterile gauze. Give a nonaspirin pain reliever.[19]
3. *Choking or blocked airway in infant under 1 year.* Assume a seated position and hold the infant facedown on your forearm, which is resting on your thigh. Thump the infant gently but firmly five times on the middle of the back using the heel of your hand. The combination of gravity and the back blows should release the blocking object. If this doesn't work, hold the infant faceup

on your forearm with the head lower than the trunk. Using two fingers placed at the center of the infant's breastbone, give five quick chest compressions.

Repeat the back blows and chest thrusts if breathing doesn't resume. Call for emergency medical help.

Begin infant CPR if one of these techniques opens the airway but the infant doesn't resume breathing.

If the child is older than age 1, give abdominal thrusts only.[20]

4. *Cuts and scrapes.* Apply pressure to stop any bleeding. Wash the affected area with soap and water. Flush out any dirt or debris. Cut off any loose pieces of skin using scissors cleaned with alcohol. Apply antibiotic ointment and cover with an adhesive bandage. Change dressing daily.[21]

5. *Bleeding.* Apply direct pressure to the wound using a clean cloth.

6. *Bloody nose.* Sit the child upright and gently lean her forward. Pinch her nose. Call the doctor if the bleeding persists for more than 20 minutes.

7. *Splinter.* Splinters can be removed in several ways. First, try using tweezers to grab the splinter by the end protruding out of the skin. Pull it out along the path that it entered. Wash the affected area with soap and water, and apply antibacterial ointment and a bandage.

For deeper splinters embedded in the skin, clean the area and a sewing needle with an antiseptic-like alcohol. Use the needle to partially dislodge the splinter, than use tweezers to remove it completely.

You can also soak the affected area in a warm water and baking soda bath twice daily. After a few days, the splinter may dislodge on its own. Call the doctor for deep splinters that you cannot remove.

8. *Tick bite.* Remove the tick by using tweezers to grasp it near its head. Try to remove the tick whole without

crushing it. Wash the area with soap and water. Call the doctor if you can't remove the tick in its entirety.

9. *Bruise.* If possible, elevate the affected area and apply ice to it several times a day for 48 hours. Give nonaspirin pain reliever, if needed. Call the doctor if your child experiences unexplained bruising or bruising accompanied by bleeding in other areas of the body.[22] Call your doctor immediately if you notice bruising around the eyes.

10. *Human bite.* Stop the bleeding by applying pressure with a clean cloth. Wash the wound with soap and water. Apply an antibiotic ointment and a bandage. Call your doctor or seek emergency medical care.

Does My Child Need Sutures?

Your child may need stitches if she has a cut that is wide or gaping open, a cut that is longer than ½ inch on the body, or a cut that is longer than ¼ inch on the face. Do not soak any wound that you think may need stitches. This can make a wound harder to close. Instead, seek emergency treatment from your child's pediatrician or local hospital.

87 CPR Instructions

Every parent and caregiver should take an annual CPR course. While there is no substitute for hands-on CPR training, the following guidelines can serve as a reminder of how to perform CPR.[23]

CPR for Infants

1. *Shout and tap.* Shout and gently tap the child on the shoulder. If there is no response, position the infant on his or her back.
2. *Open the airway.* Open the airway using a head tilt lifting of chin. Do not tilt the head too far back.
3. *Give two gentle breaths.* If the baby is *not* breathing, give two small gentle breaths. Cover the baby's mouth and nose with your mouth. Each breath should be 1 second long. You should see the baby's chest rise with each breath.
4. *Give thirty compressions.* Give thirty gentle chest compressions at the rate of 100 per minute. Use two or three fingers in the center of the chest just below the nipples. Press down approximately one-third the depth of the chest.
5. *Repeat.* Repeat with two breaths and thirty compressions. After two minutes of repeated cycles, call 911 and continue giving breaths and compressions.

CPR for Children Ages 1–8

CPR for children is similar to CPR for adults. For children, the compression to ventilation ratio is 30:2. There are, however, three differences.

1. If you are alone with the child, give two minutes of CPR before calling 911.
2. Use the heel of one or two hands for chest compressions.
3. Press the sternum approximately one-third the depth of the chest.

Family and Friends CPR Anytime

The American Heart Association has developed a training program that can teach families the basics of CPR in about 20 minutes from the comfort of their own homes. Complete with a learning DVD and an inflatable manikin with accessories, the program is available to teach both infant and adult/child CPR skills. Visit www.heart.org for more information.

88 What Belongs in a First Aid Kit?

A well-stocked first aid kit is a must for every home and automobile. First aid kits should have the necessary supplies to stop bleeding, to clean wounds, and to prevent infection. Pack a lightweight compartmentalized plastic container with the following items. Clearly label your container as a first aid kit and store it out of the reach of children.

emergency information and contact list
first aid manual

assortment of adhesive bandages
assortment of sterile and nonsterile gauze squares
blister pads
butterfly wound closures
hypoallergenic medical tape
self-adhering elastic bandage roll
roll of gauze

antibiotic ointment
antihistamine
anti-itch cream
antiseptic hand gel
antiseptic wipes
antiseptic wound spray
burn ointment
calamine lotion
extra prescription medications
eyewash
hydrocortisone
nonaspirin pain reliever
petroleum jelly

CPR mouthpiece barrier
digital thermometer
instant ice pack
latex-free gloves
mini flashlight
safety pins
small scissors
thermometer probe covers
tweezers

Hold It!

Tackle boxes, plastic containers designed to hold art supplies, or other compartmentalized, handled, plastic containers are perfect for storing first aid supplies. Fanny packs are great for storing first aid supplies while hiking or on a day trip.

89 Emergency Information You Should Always Have on Hand

During an emergency, you may not be able to clearly communicate vital information about your children to medical responders. For this reason, it can be beneficial to keep a list of emergency information easily accessible and in a place where others might look for it. You'll also want to be sure that anyone caring for your child has this information as well.

Emergency information that you should always keep on hand for each child includes:

- child's name
- address
- phone number
- date of birth
- recent picture
- current height and weight
- insurance card or copy
- health conditions
- current medications
- allergies
- physician
- hospital of choice
- name and contact number for parents
- emergency contact number for an additional family member
- emergency contact number for a nonfamily member

Safety First

In an emergency situation, it can be easy to forget even the simplest details. Use a basic computer program to generate an emergency contact card for each child. The above information, a recent picture, and the date that the card was made should be included. These can be easily laminated by purchasing plastic sheets at your local office store. Tape a card to each child's car seat and to the front of your fridge. You'll also want to keep one card in your wallet and place one in the glove box of your vehicle.

Identification Cards from Local Police

Local police stations often provide child identification safety cards to parents in their community. These cards contain emergency information, identifying information, and often fingerprints of your child. Contact your local police station to see if they provide this free community resource.

90 Acetaminophen and Ibuprofen Dosage Charts for Children

When your child has a fever over 100.2 degrees, you may wish to give him an over the counter medicine to make him feel more comfortable. But just because over the counter medications are readily available, they should not be used without caution. When used properly, acetaminophen and ibuprofen can help soothe your child's aches and pains and reduce fever, but be sure to read all labels carefully and consult with your pediatrician before dispensing any medication to a child younger than 3 months of age.

Ibuprofen versus Acetaminophen

According to the American Academy of Pediatrics, "Ibuprofen tends to work better than acetaminophen in treating high fevers (103° F or higher)." But ibuprofen should not be given to children younger than 6 months or children who are dehydrated or vomiting.[24]

What Constitutes a Fever?

	Oral	Rectal
Normal temperature	98.6	99.6
Fever	99.4	100.4

Acetaminophen Dosage Chart

Dosages of acetaminophen may be repeated every 4 hours but should not be given more than 5 times in 24 hours. (*Note: milliliter* is abbreviated as ml; 5 ml equals 1 teaspoon [tsp.]. A household teaspoon should not be used to administer medication because they can vary widely in size. Instead use the measuring tool that came with the medication or a syringe or spoon designed for administering medication.) The American Academy of Pediatrics does *not* recommend using aspirin to treat a simple fever.[25]

Age	Weight	Drops 80 mg/ 0.8 ml	Elixir 160 mg/ 5 ml	Chewable Tablets 80 mg tablets
0–3 months	6–11 lbs. (2.7–5 kg)	0.4 ml	—	—
4–11 months	12–17 lbs. (5.5–7.7 kg)	0.8 ml	½ tsp.	1 tablet
1–2 years	18–23 lbs. (8.2–10.5 kg)	1.2 ml	¾ tsp.	1½ tablets
2–3 years	24–35 lbs. (10.9–15.9 kg)	1.6 ml	1 tsp.	2 tablets
4–5 years	36–47 lbs. (16.3–21.4 kg)	2.4 ml	1½ tsp.	3 tablets

273

Ibuprofen Dosage Chart

Dosages of ibuprofen may be repeated every 6 to 8 hours but should not be given more than 4 times in 24 hours. (*Note: milliliter* is abbreviated as ml; 5 ml equals 1 teaspoon [tsp.]. Don't use household teaspoons, which can vary in size.) The American Academy of Pediatrics does *not* recommend using aspirin to treat a simple fever. [26]

Age*	Weight†	Drops 40 mg/ 1.5 ml	Elixir 100 mg/ 5 ml	Chewable Tablets 50 mg tablets
6–11 months	12–17 lbs. (5.5–7.7 kg)	1 dropper	—	—
1–2 years	18–23 lbs. (8.2–10.5 kg)	1½ droppers	—	—
2–3 years	24–35 lbs. (10.9–15.9 kg)	2 droppers	1 tsp.	—
4–5 years	36–47 lbs. (16.3–21.4 kg)	—	1½ tsp.	3 tablets

*Note: age is provided as a convenience only. Dosing for fever should be based on baseline weight.

†Weight given is representative of the age range.

When Your Child Is Sick

- Don't be afraid to call the doctor if you are unsure about administering over the counter medications. If you are unsure, always call the doctor before giving any medication.
- Always call the doctor if your child is lethargic, unresponsive, refusing to eat, has a rash, is having difficulty breathing, or if your child's fever has lasted more than a few days.
- Most pediatricians' offices have a "nurse's line" that you can call and ask questions. Take advantage of this helpful resource.

- Keep track of your child's temperature, using a digital thermometer, and keep track of the times you give fever reducer and the amount. This prevents accidental overdose and provides an easy way for you to monitor closely your child's fever.
- If your child is younger than 2–4 months and has a fever, always call the doctor right away.

Three Rules to Prevent a Medication Mix-Up

When it comes to kids and medication, always follow these three rules:

1. Listen to the instructions of the prescribing doctor and repeat back to the doctor the medication name and dosing instructions. If your doctor seems rushed or if you're preoccupied with the kids, ask the doctor to slow down or to write the instructions out for you.
2. Look at the label. Be sure it's yours and confirm that the label matches the instructions the prescribing doctor gave you. Always check your prescriptions before leaving the store.
3. Ask for clarification. Speak up if things don't make sense, and take advantage of the pharmacist consult that most pharmacies offer. Be sure to speak to the pharmacist, not the technician, if you do have questions. If you are given a syringe to administer medication and the units on it don't match the units on your label, ask for a different measuring tool or for the conversion amounts.

91 The Top Twelve Safety Mistakes Parents Make

Some mistakes you can learn from, but when it comes to your children, you don't want to take the chance.

1. *Buying the wrong car seat, installing the car seat incorrectly, or failing to use a car seat when one is needed.* Seven out of ten children in car seats are not properly restrained. Children should ride in the backseat of the vehicle in a rear-facing child safety seat until they have reached the maximum height and weight recommended for the model, or at least until age 2.[27] Children should ride in a forward-facing safety seat until they weigh 40 pounds, and they should be in a booster seat until they turn 8. Children 4 feet, 9 inches tall should properly fit in a seat belt. Children should ride in the backseat until age 13.[28]

2. *Using a crib that fails to meet the standards of the United States Consumer Product Safety Commission.* Cribs should not have slats that are more than 2⅜ inches apart, corner posts more than 1/16 of an inch high, and any cutouts in the headboard or footboard. Do not use old cribs or hand-me-downs that don't meet these standards.

3. *Keeping the baby's room too hot or too cold.* A baby's room should be "comfortable to a lightly clothed adult."[29] This temperature usually falls between 60 and 70 degrees Fahrenheit.

4. *Sharing your bed with baby.* The American Academy of Pediatrics recommends that babies sleep in separate, but close sleeping areas. Babies can easily suffocate or

become entrapped in an adult bed. Instead, opt for a co-sleeping bassinet that attaches securely to the side of an adult bed.

5. *Putting your baby to sleep on her stomach, instead of her back.* To reduce the risk of sudden infant death syndrome, babies should always be put to sleep on their back.

6. *Failing to lower the water heater thermostat.* To prevent burning, your water heater thermostat should be set no higher than 120 degrees Fahrenheit. Temperatures higher than that can burn a child in a matter of seconds.

7. *Failing to perform background and reference checks on potential child care providers.* Although it can be tempting to go with your gut, you really need to know who's caring for your child. Many online companies provide Internet-based background checks. You can find a credible company on the International Nanny Association website (http://www.nanny.org/).

8. *Not completing a CPR and first aid course.* Being prepared for an emergency can literally mean the difference between life and death. Contact your local chapter of the American Red Cross or the American Heart Association to find a course near you.

9. *Feeding a child inappropriate foods that can cause choking.* Carrots, raisins, celery, chips, popcorn, peanut butter, hotdogs, grapes, nuts, hard candy, and gum should be fed to children with extreme caution.

10. *Placing poisons within a child's reach.* Medications, vitamins, herbal supplements, cleaners, and chemicals should always be stored out of the reach of children.

11. *Leaving kids alone in the car.* Children should never be left alone in a vehicle for any amount of time, even if they can be clearly seen from where you're going (like an ATM). Kids can quickly become overheated,

can accidentally put a car into gear, can be victims of a crime, or get into other safety trouble.

12. *Improper supervision while bathing.* Children can drown in an inch of water in a matter of seconds. Don't let bath rings or other bathing devices give you a false sense of security. Never leave your baby unattended while bathing.

Safety Stats

- In a vehicle crash at 30 miles per hour, an unbelted child would hit the dashboard with as much force as a fall from a three-story building.[30]
- Since the beginning of the American Academy of Pediatrics Back to Sleep campaign, the SIDS rate has dropped 38 percent.[31]
- An estimated 70 percent of accidental poisonings are preventable.[32]
- Between 1990 and 1997, at least 515 deaths for children under age 2 were related to sleeping in adult beds.[33]

92 Childproofing 101

Each year 4.5 million children are injured inside of their own homes.[34] While there is no substitute for vigilant supervision, childproofing your home can help protect your children from accidental injury. Consider using these childproofing measures in your home.

Throughout the House

- Use latches and safety locks for cabinets and drawers that contain chemicals, cleaners, medications, sharp objects, or other items that are unsafe for children to prevent injury and poisoning.

- Use safety gates to block access to stairwells and other unsafe areas of the home to prevent injury and falls. Use expansion gates to prevent access to fireplaces and use gates that have hardware installation for the top of staircases.

- Use doorknob covers and door locks to prevent access into off-limit rooms.

- Turn the water heater to below 120 degrees Fahrenheit to prevent accidental burns.

- Use working smoke detectors to alert the family to fire.

- Use carbon monoxide detectors throughout the home to prevent carbon monoxide poisoning.

- Lock firearms and keep ammunition stored separately to prevent accidental injury.

- Unplug appliances when not in use to prevent injury.

- Store magnets and small batteries out of the reach of children to prevent choking.

- Always opt for child-resistant tops on medications to prevent accidental poisoning.

- Store plastic bags in a locked drawer or cabinet and tie several knots in them before throwing them away to prevent suffocation.

- Avoid toy chests that have lids to prevent injury and entrapment.

- Gather up long appliance cords and secure with a twist tie to prevent children from pulling or chewing on the cord.

- Install window guards, locks, and stoppers to prevent accidental falls from windows that children can open.
- Use doorstops to prevent injuries to fingers.
- Choose furniture with smooth wood to prevent splinters.
- Use netting on banister rails on stairwells, decks, and in foyers to prevent accidental entrapment.
- Use cord tassels or winders to prevent strangulation from window blind cords.
- Use cordless phones to prevent accidental strangulation from phone cords.
- Use corner and edge bumpers on anything sharp to prevent injuries caused from falls.
- Use outlet covers to prevent electrocution. Opt for a sliding outlet cover, rather than the plastic outlet plugs that can easily end up in a child's mouth.
- Attach furniture to walls to prevent knock-over accidents.
- Avoid furniture with decorative cutouts where a child's limbs could be caught.
- Use rug pads underneath loose rugs to prevent injuries from slipping, tripping, and falling.

In the Bathroom

- Place a plastic guard over tub spout to prevent burns and injury.
- Apply a nonskid surface to bathtubs and shower stalls to prevent slips and falls.
- Use a toilet lid lock to prevent accidental drowning.
- Install grounded circuit breakers in the bathroom to prevent electrocution.

In the Kitchen

- Use knob covers to prevent access to stove knobs.
- Use locks to prevent access to appliances. You can purchase locks specifically designed for refrigerators, dishwashers, and more.
- Remove tablecloths and placemats to reduce the risk of injury that can result in a child pulling them off the table and spilling hot liquids or heavy or sharp tableware on himself.
- Cook on back stove burners with pot handles turned in to prevent access to hot pans.

In the Nursery

- Only use a crib that has slats no more than $2\frac{3}{8}$ inches apart to prevent entrapment or strangulation.
- Corner posts or finials of beds and cribs should be no higher than $\frac{1}{16}$ of an inch, and no shorter than 16 inches if it holds a canopy, to prevent injury.
- Avoid using bumpers or putting fluffy bedding or stuffed toys in children's sleeping areas.

Outdoors

- Use tall, locked gates to prevent access to pools to prevent accidental drowning.
- Be sure outdoor play equipment is in good shape and check for loose bolts or sharp edges to prevent injury.
- Choose loose fill surfaces like mulch, sand, or rubber for play areas. Use fill that is 12 inches deep and that extends a minimum of 6 feet past play equipment to offer the best protection from falls.

- Always empty buckets and kiddie pools to prevent accidental drowning.

To Get Perspective

Always get down on your hands and knees to see your child's view of the home. Look for items that could cause injury and take appropriate measures to create a safe environment for your child.

Things to Avoid

Infant walkers. Between 1990 and 2001 approximately 197,200 infants under 15 months of age were treated in U.S. emergency room departments for infant walker-related injuries. Some of these injuries even resulted in death.[35] Common injuries included falls, pinched fingers and toes, and injuries resulting from the infant's increased mobility and ability to get into unsafe places. Instead, choose a stationary saucer.
Drawstring clothing. Avoid dressing your child in clothing with drawstrings. Drawstrings can get caught on or around things and result in injury or strangulation.

93 Hidden Household Poisons

Many items and products commonly found in the household can pose a significant poisoning risk to children. Take proper measures to store the following items and products securely and always keep them out of the reach of children.

herbal supplements

nonprescription medications, including diet pills, supplements, vitamins, and decongestants

prescription medications

ammonia

bleach

dishwasher detergent

drain declogger

furniture polish

laundry detergent

oven cleaner

antifreeze

bug spray

gasoline

kerosene

lighter fluid

paint thinner

rust remover

windshield wiper fluid

aftershave

cologne

hair relaxer

mouthwash

nail polish

nail polish remover

perm products

arts and crafts supplies

batteries

beer, wine, and liquor

houseplants

plant food

Common Poisonous Household Plants

aloe vera

amaryllis

angel's trumpet

angels' wings

azalea

ceriman

croton

crown of thorns

cyclamen

devil's backbone

dumb cane

English ivy

flamingo lily

hydrangea

Jerusalem cherry

mums

philodendron

poinsettia[36]

283

In Case of Poisoning

If you suspect that your child has been exposed to a poison, call the American Association of Poison Control Centers at 800-222-1222 immediately. Be prepared to tell them what you think your child came in contact with, how she was exposed (by eating, drinking, smelling, or touching), if she's vomited, and her age, height, and weight.

Keep ipecac syrup and activated charcoal on hand, but *use only* if specifically directed by the poison control center.

If you are told to seek medical treatment, take the suspected poison with you.

Bye-Bye Baby Powder

Baby powder is a no-no. The initial "poof" of small powder particles from a baby powder container can be inhaled and cause lung damage, respiratory issues, or aspiration. Even though many companies have replaced talc with cornstarch as a main ingredient in baby powder, inhaling any type of powder particles isn't good. Instead, choose a diaper ointment to protect your baby's bottom.

Poison Prevention

- Choose child-resistant caps on medications and be sure to put them on securely after each use.
- Store poisonous products in the containers that they came in. Never use food containers to store poisonous products.
- Store cleaning products away from food products.

- Keep medications and other household poisons securely stored and out of the reach of children.
- Never mix cleaning products together.
- Buy only nontoxic arts and crafts supplies.
- Don't give your child expired medications or medication not intended for her or her current condition.

94 Home Hazards

There are many obvious hazards located inside and around the home, but there are some other dangers that pose a significant threat to the health and safety of children that aren't quite so obvious. Here are fifty of them.

Top Five Hidden Hazards

The United States Consumer Product Safety Commission says the top five hidden hazards of the home are:

1. magnets
2. recalled products*
3. furniture that can tip over
4. windows and window treatments
5. pool and spa drains[37]

*Visit the United States Consumer Product Safety Commission website at http://www.cpsc.gov/ to learn about product recalls.

Fifty Household Hazards Found inside and around the Home

1. adult beds used for co-sleeping
2. appliances
3. asbestos
4. baby walkers
5. BBQ grills
6. bleach cleaning products
7. broken play equipment
8. broken smoke and carbon monoxide detectors
9. buckets filled with water
10. burning candles
11. button batteries
12. cleaning products with bleach
13. coin-size foods
14. crib bumpers
15. decks
16. fertilizer
17. firearms
18. fish ponds
19. frayed wires
20. garage doors
21. gardening supplies and equipment
22. gasoline
23. glass Christmas tree ornaments
24. heated stove tops and food cooking on them
25. infant bathing seats
26. kiddie pools
27. lawn mowers
28. lead paint
29. loose blankets, pillows, or toys in crib
30. matches
31. medications
32. mercury thermometers
33. mold

34. mushrooms
35. overloaded plug sockets
36. paint thinner
37. pesticides
38. plants
39. plastic bags
40. poisonous plants
41. pools
42. radon
43. space heaters
44. stairways not properly gated
45. supplies and equipment for home repair
46. tap water*
47. toy chests
48. unsecured televisions and bureaus
49. vitamins
50. window blind cords

*Set your water heater thermostat to no higher than 120 degrees F to prevent burns.

LIST
95 Choking Hazards

To reduce the risk of choking, carefully monitor your child when eating the following foods and playing with the following items. Always be sure to cut foods into small pieces before serving to your child to reduce choking risks. Hot dogs should be sliced lengthwise, then cut, and grapes should be quartered before serving to young children.

candy—hard, gooey, or
 sticky
chewing gum
fruit, dried
fruit, hard, in chunks
grapes, whole
hot dogs
marshmallows
meat or cheese in chunks
nuts and seeds
peanut butter
popcorn
potato chips
pretzels
veggies, raw

balloons

balls, small
batteries, small button-
 type
bulbs to medicine
 syringes
buttons
coins
ice cubes
Lego toys
magnets
marbles
pen or marker caps
toys that can be squeezed
 to fit entirely into a
 child's mouth
toys with small parts
water or soda bottle caps

If You Suspect Your Child Is Choking

When food goes down the wrong pipe, a child can appear
to be choking. But if he is coughing and can speak, he is not
choking. In this case, encourage him to continue to cough to
free the food that has gone down the wrong pipe. If a child
turns blue, cannot speak, begins breathing heavily, or gag-
ging, he may be choking.[38]

If your child is older than 1 and is choking, follow these
steps recommended by the American Heart Association.[39]

1. If you think a child is choking, ask the child, "Are you
   choking?" If he nods, tell him you are going to help.
2. Kneel or stand firmly behind him and wrap your arms
   around him so that your hands are in front.
3. Make a fist with one hand.

4. Put the thumb side of your fist slightly above the navel (belly button) and well below the breastbone.
5. Grasp the fist with your other hand and give quick upward thrusts into his abdomen.
6. Give thrusts until the object is forced out and he can breathe, cough, or talk or until he stops responding.

Always call emergency services or 911 if you are concerned about your child's status.

Tips to Prevent Choking

- Children younger than 4 years of age are still learning to chew and grind their food. For this reason, children younger than 4 should never be fed round, firm foods, unless they are chopped or completely ground.
- Follow the recommendations on children's toy packaging. They are provided to protect your child from choking or injury.
- Keep a close eye on older children. Many choking incidents occur when older siblings unknowingly give dangerous foods, toys, or small objects to their younger siblings.

Universal Sign for Choking

Teach your child the universal sign for choking, which is a hand clutching the throat, with thumb and fingers extended.

Infant Choking

Back blows or chest thrusts are used to dislodge an object from a choking infant. If your baby becomes unconscious at any time, infant CPR should be given (see List 87).[40]

96 Questions to Ask When Interviewing a Child Care Provider

Choosing a child care provider can be an issue of mother's instinct, but even if your gut says yes, it's important to conduct a thorough interview with any potential child care provider.

A Nanny or Babysitter

If interviewing a nanny or babysitter, be sure to ask:

Why do you enjoy working with children?

Why did you choose to work in a private home rather than a center?

Are you available to work the hours that I am offering?

Are you CPR and first aid certified?

What is your experience? Ask follow-up questions relevant to the type of experience you expect a qualified candidate to have. For example, if you have a child with special needs, ask if the candidate has experience with special needs children.

What is your education?

Do you drive?

Do you have a reliable vehicle?

Do you hold any child care credentials or certifications?

What is your salary range?

Will you submit to a background check?

Can I check your driving record?

Are you a member of any professional organizations?

When are you available to start?

Are you flexible with scheduling?

When do you plan on taking vacation?

Do you like to pick up additional hours for additional pay?

Are you willing to travel with our family?

How do you feel about light housekeeping?

Can you prepare meals for my children?

What was your last child care experience like? Why did you leave?

How long are you planning to stay at your next job?

Are you willing to make a one-year commitment?

What is your parenting philosophy?

What methods of discipline do you use?

What would a typical day caring for children be like?

How do you feel about kids and TV?

Do you develop a routine for the children? Are you structured?

What do kids like best about you?

What kind of activities do you do with children the ages of mine?

How do you handle a baby that is crying inconsolably?

How do you handle a temper tantrum?

Are you willing to take my children to age-appropriate activities and outings?

What is your relationship with your family like?

With whom do you spend most of your time?

How do people describe you?

Do you have any special skills?

Do you have any habits I should know about? What do you do for fun?

Do you have any habits that may negatively influence my children?

Can I have information for contacting three references?

If you are hiring a live-in caregiver, be sure to ask these additional questions:

What time do you usually go to bed?

Do you usually stay out past midnight on weekends?

Have you lived with a family before?

Do you have any special conditions or preferences I should know about?

Do you plan to entertain in your area of the house?

Warning Signs

While every mom should trust their gut when it comes to choosing child care, there are some things that should raise a red flag when interviewing a potential caregiver.

Proceed with caution if the candidate:

- is hesitant about giving contact information for references
- can't legitimately explain gaps in employment
- can't produce a valid drivers liscence or other form of government issued identification
- does not have a social security number
- refuses to provide written consent for a criminal background check
- requests that employment taxes not be withheld from their pay

Tips for Hiring an In-home Child Care Provider

- *Know the difference between a nanny and a babysitter.* According to the International Nanny Association, a babysitter "provides supervisory, custodial care of children on an irregular full-time or part-time basis," while a nanny is "employed by the family on either a live-in or live-out basis to undertake all tasks related to the care of children" for forty to sixty hours per week. While a babysitter is not expected to have much experience or formal training, a nanny usually has an educational background in child care and extensive experience working with children.

- *Know your responsibilities.* Nannies and babysitters are not independent contractors. Nanny employers are required to file employment taxes and are subject to federal and state employment laws.

- *Always schedule a trial period.* A trial period provides a time frame for you to be sure that the quality of care your child is receiving is meeting your expectations. Use this time to observe your provider in action.

A Child Care Center

If interviewing a child care center, be sure to ask:

Does the facility do a background check on all employees?

Is the center licensed and accredited?[41]

How long has the center been open?

Does the center have a religious affiliation?

What is the center's philosophy on discipline and on learning?

Do you have an open-door policy for parents (parents can visit at any time)?

293

How many and what are the ages of the children in the program?

What hours is child care available?

What is the cost of care?

What are the penalties for early drop-off or late pickup?

What meals or snacks do you provide?

What do I have to supply for my child?

What is the ratio of adults to children?

What is the staff turnover rate?

What is the experience and education of the staff?

Is your staff required to have current CPR and first aid certification?

Do you have backup if a teacher is sick?

Do you operate on the public school schedule?

What is the center's closing policy? How do you notify parents?

What is your "sick kid" policy?

What would a typical day for my child be like? Is there a structured schedule?

Do the children play outside each day?

Do you have a safe, enclosed outdoor play area?

Do children watch TV?

Do children nap?

How do you feed infants? Do you prop bottles? How do you warm the bottles?

What is your policy on toileting? Do children have to be toilet trained?

Do you transport the children on field trips? Who drives? What vehicle is used? Are there safety seats?

How often are babies held?

How do you handle an aggressive child?

How do you handle separation anxiety?

What security measures are used?

What is your policy on nonparent pickup?

What are the emergency procedures?

What situation would precipitate a phone call home?

What is your policy on administering medications?

Are you peanut free?

What are your cleaning procedures? What chemicals do you use and how often do you use them?

What is your termination of enrollment policy?

Do you have the name of three families I can call for references?

If considering a family day care that operates inside a private home or if you are considering taking your child to a caregiver's home, also ask:

Who has access to the home?

Who will be coming and going from the premises when the children are present?

Is there someone who provides coverage if you are sick or closed?

What is the maximum number of children allowed in your program?

Do you have assistants?

Warning Signs

When evaluating child care centers, the following red flags may alert you to potential issues within the center:

• A high staff turnover rate. May signify staff isn't paid or treated well.

- Lack of a written policy and procedures manual. May signify that there are no set standards that govern the operations of the center.
- Safety issues with the building or play structures. May signify safety isn't the center's first priority.
- Refusal to provide family references. May signify that past clients won't give a positive review.
- A closed door policy. May signify that when parents are not present the staff does things differently.

Child to Child Care Staff Ratios

The American Academy of Pediatrics recommends the following guidelines for child to staff ratios:

Age of Child	Child to Staff Ratio	Maximum Group Size
Birth–24 months	3:1	5
25–30 months	4:1	8
31–35 months	5:1	10
3 years	7:1	14
4–5 years	8:1	16

LISTS FOR SAVING YOUR TIME, MONEY, AND 'SANITY'

97 Baby on a Budget

According to the 2007 United States Department of Agriculture annual "Expenditures on Children by Families" report, married couples can expect to spend between $7,830 and $16,290 per year, per child the first two years of life.[1] Ouch! Raising a child is expensive! In addition to breastfeeding, which will provide you with significant savings, there are other cost-saving measures that can make the first year of childrearing a bit easier on the wallet.

Ten Savings Tips for the First Year

1. *Cut back on the nursery decor.* While the comforter set and the bumpers are cute, they're really unnecessary, not to mention unsafe. To prevent suffocation and SIDS, never put a baby to bed with loose blankets. Bumpers can pose a suffocation risk as well, since babies often snuggle up close to them. And the crib skirt is cute to look at but impractical, as it can easily get caught when raising and lowering the crib rail.
   Savings: $100–400.
2. *Skip the changing table.* Instead of purchasing a changing table, get yourself a small waterproof pad to use on the floor.
   Savings: $50–150.
3. *Sign up for a formula company–sponsored baby club.* Signing up for a baby club can almost guarantee you'll

299

get monthly coupons. Similac's Strong Moms club, for example, sends five $5 coupons when you sign up and then one $5 coupon each month.
Savings: $85 the first year.

4. *Make your own baby food.* According to Gerber, babies eat, on average, six hundred jars of baby food or fruit juice during their first year of life.[2] A 2.5-ounce jar of Gerber peas costs about 59 cents, or about 23 cents per ounce. A 16-ounce bag of frozen peas costs 89 cents or 4 cents an ounce.[3]
Savings: $294 per year.

5. *Shop the off-season sales.* You can actually purchase quality, brand-name clothing for less than you'd pay at a consignment shop if you shop the end-of-season clearance racks. Often Macy's has a wide selection of brand-name clothing for pennies on the dollar. Recently I purchased a dress priced at $19.95 for $2.50. That's nearly 90 percent off the original price!
Savings: 60–90 percent of original price.

6. *Stick with the essentials.* Limiting your nonessential purchases can save you big time. It's tempting to purchase both a swing and a bouncing seat for your baby, but he really needs only one of those. Limit gizmos and gadgets and you'll really save.
Savings: $50 and more.

7. *Accept hand-me-downs.* They are a great way to save. From clothes to equipment, you can save hundreds when you don't have to buy these things. Wash clothing and wipe down gear before you use it. Since most baby items are used for only a short time, chances are most things will come to you in good condition or can be made to look like new pretty easily.
Savings: $100 and more.

8. *Clip coupons.* Look for coupons for formula, diapers, baby food, and other necessities in your local store cir-

culars, on manufacturer's websites, and in the kits new moms often receive from the hospital or in the mail. Savings: $1.00–$5.00 per purchase.

9. *Choose a convertible crib.* You may spend a few more dollars up front, but in the long run you'll save money. There are 3-in-1 cribs that go from crib to daybed or toddler bed and 4-in-1 cribs that go from crib to daybed or toddler bed to an adult sized bed. In most cases, you'll need to purchase the mattress separately. Savings: $100–400 over lifetime of use.

10. *Buy disposable diapers in bulk when on sale.* Although this may not appear to produce tons of savings, over the course of the year, it can add up to quite a significant amount. Just saving 5 cents per diaper can add up to an annual savings of $120.[4] Savings: $100–150 per year.

How Much Does It Cost to Raise a Child?

The total average cost of raising a child in the United States until the age of seventeen is between $148,320 and $298,680.[5]

98 Ten Time-Management Tips for Moms

More time, more energy, and more relaxation are at the top of every mother's wish list. Fortunately, mothers who have good time-management skills *do* find more time in their day and feel less stressed and more productive overall. Implement these time-management tips in your day and you'll be amazed at how quickly your week is transformed.

1. *Have a routine*. Having a predictable, structured day can help assure that you complete and streamline your daily tasks, saving you buckets of time over the course of the day.
2. *Be organized*. Being organized helps you keep track of important information and items and avoids time-consuming hunts for an item or information you need.
3. *Have a place for everything*. This encourages the habit of putting things back where they came from and picking up as you go along, eliminating an extensive end-of-the-day cleanup.
4. *Use a family calendar*. Having a family calendar with you at all times can help keep everyone's social commitments in order, avoiding overscheduling. You'll save time because you won't have to return calls to confirm plans or cancel double booking.
5. *Keep a daily to-do list*. Having a running to-do list can keep important jobs front and center, so that when you have an extra nugget of time, you can tackle a task on your list.
6. *Delegate*. Delegating tasks and responsibilities to others can save you tons of time. Having older kids help out with chores and outsourcing domestic tasks to others can save you hours of time each week.
7. *Learn to say no*. Saying no to invitations, additional responsibilities, and commitments you know you can't keep can save you time instantaneously.
8. *Prioritize*. When you prioritize items in your days, weeks, and months, you are better able to focus on the items that need to be done, saving you from having to crunch to meet deadlines and obligations.
9. *Keep a running grocery list*. Write things down as you run out of them, so you're sure to pick them up when needed. Doing so can save you from having to make multiple trips to the store.

10. *Plan a weekly menu.* Deciding what to make for dinner is one of the most time-consuming tasks of many a mother's day. Sitting down one night a week to plan out your menu and writing out your shopping list can save you precious time each day.

Top Time-Saving Tip

Set your alarm to wake up a half hour before your kids so you can shower and prepare for your day before they get up. Then when the troops rise, you can focus on getting them ready and out the door.

99 Twenty-five Quick, Easy, and Affordable Home Organization Ideas

1. Use ice cube trays to sort and store small items like screws or buttons.
2. Use baskets to organize and store kids' toys.
3. Toss spare change into a glass vase.
4. Sort and store photos chronologically in shoe boxes.
5. Purchase interlocking organizers for kitchen drawers.
6. Use formula canisters to store crayons, bottle nipples, or other small items.
7. Reuse plastic baby wipe containers to store plastic grocery bags.
8. Store elastics or hair bands on an empty toilet paper roll.
9. Use baby food jars to store pushpins, paper clips, or other small office supplies.

10. Hang a plastic shoe organizer on the back of the door to store children's hats, mittens, or small toys.

11. Tuck a small wastebasket in a hall closet to hold umbrellas.

12. Place a hook on the back of each bedroom door to hold nightgowns and pajamas.

13. Use an office-size wastebasket to hold wrapping paper rolls and supplies.

14. Save zip-up soft plastic packaging to store clothes your child has outgrown.

15. Use a large plastic cup or decorative mug to hold pens and pencils.

16. Place a muffin tin in your nightstand drawer to sort necklaces, change, spare buttons, and other small items.

17. Hang hooks in your closets, pantries, and in stairwells to hold brooms, dustpans, or aprons.

18. Use film canisters to store small items like beads, safety pins, or super glue tubes.

19. Use a large plastic laundry tub as a toy box in the living room.

20. Use a lazy Susan to organize and store jars of baby food.

21. Put kids' silverware in a separate utensil tray.

22. Use a tackle box to organize and store your daughter's hair accessories.

23. Use a canvas bag to tote and store library books.

24. Place small plastic baskets in bathroom closets and drawers to hold toothpaste, ointments, and lotions.

25. Reuse glass canisters to hold candies and other special treats.

Overwhelmed with Disorganization?

- Start organizing a small space. A drawer, a closet, or a pantry is a good place to start.

- Remember, be slow and steady. Inch by inch, anything's a cinch!
- Don't give up! Visualize your organized space and take joy in your small organizational accomplishments to help push you toward completion.

100 Best Bargain Shops

Every area of the country is home to stores that offer significant discounts and savings, but the following chain stores boast significant savings on certain categories of items that make them well worth a trip.

Store	Save On
The Dollar Tree, Family Dollar, Ocean State Job Lot	cards, paper products, office supplies, kids' books
T.J. Maxx, Marshalls, Ross Dress for Less, Burlington Coat Factory	designer clothing for the family, toys, books
HomeGoods	home decor items, upscale kids' toys, personalized kids' art, baskets, kitchenware, frames
Carter's Outlet, OshKosh B'Gosh Outlet	baby and young children's clothing
Super Target , Wal-Mart Supercenter	groceries, paper products
A.C. Moore	frames, baskets
Christmas Tree Shops	baskets, bins
Kohl's	family clothing
DSW, Payless, Filene's Basement, Marshalls	family shoes

Reward Programs

Take advantage of the reward programs that stores offer. Often stores send members coupons, in addition to providing them in-store savings, cash rebates, and an annual cash percentage of the money that they've spent.

Onward to Outlets

Often retail and catalog outlet stores provide substantial discounts. Look for coupons to double up on your savings.

101 Ten Terrific Tips That Save Time *and* Money

For busy moms, saving time and money is always welcomed, but some techniques just take too long to be worth putting them into practice. Have no fear; effortless tips are here! Check out these top tips that will surely save you time and money.

1. *Always shop with a list.* You'll save time and money by purchasing only the items you went to the store to get.
2. *Use multipurpose beauty products.* With items like all-in-one shampoos and powder foundations, you'll need to buy only one product, cutting your cost and application time in half.
3. *Pay bills online.* Click your way to savings by paying your bills online. You'll eliminate the cost of stamps and a trip to the post office.
4. *Enroll in automatic bill pay.* This way you won't have to write out checks each month, buy stamps, or ever encounter late fees again.

5. *Double your meals.* Buy the ingredients to your favorite meals in bulk and make double the recipe. Freeze one batch and you'll have an already prepared meal ready to go.

6. *Get cash back.* Avoid trips to the ATM and excessive withdrawal fees by utilizing the cash back feature when you're paying for goods at a store.

7. *Shop online.* When you know what you want, find it and get it at the price you want to pay by shopping online.

8. *Stock up on sale items.* Buying toilet paper, paper towels, or other home necessities in bulk when they're on sale can save you from having to pay full price and from making extra trips to the store.

9. *Sign up for grocery store rewards.* Clipping coupons can be tedious work, but signing up for a store rewards card can usually get you the sale prices with the swipe of your card.

10. *Combine your services.* Investigate combining your cable, Internet, phone, and cell phone services. You'll usually get a reduced rate and you'll have only one bill.

Stretch Your Dollar

Visit the website of the Dollar Stretcher at www.stretcher .com for tips and daily updates on how to live better for less.

Look for Discounts

• Ask your household service providers if they extend a discount for up-front payment. Some service providers offer discounts if you pay for your services by the year.

• Keep current on the specials. Many companies offer new subscribers significant savings. If you're an established customer, they'll often extend you the same discount if you ask.

• Ask for a rate reduction. If you have good credit, your credit company may honor your request to decrease your interest rate. Ask what the current rates are and if there is any room for a rate reduction on your account.

102 Common Clothing Size Guidelines for the First Years

Children's clothing sizes can vary from manufacturer to manufacturer because there is no industry standard. When purchasing children's clothing, it's always best to use the manufacturer's length and weight measurement recommendations, usually printed on the garments' tags.

Carter's Clothing

Size	Weight in Pounds	Length in Inches
Preemie	0–5	17
Newborn	5–8	21.5
3 months	8–12.5	21.5–24
6 months	12.5–16.5	24–26.5
9 months	16.5–20.5	26.5–28.5
12 months	20.5–24.5	28.5–30.5
18 months	24.5–27.5	30.5–32.5
24 months	27.5–30	32.5–34
2T	29–31	34.5–36.5
3T	31–34	36.5–38.5
4T	34–38	38.5–41.5

Size	Weight in Pounds	Length in Inches
5T	38–42	41.5–43.5
4	37–39	40–42.5
5	39–44	42.5–45
6	44–49	45–48
6x	49–55	48–50.5

Gap Clothing

Size	Weight in Pounds	Length in Inches
Preemie	up to 5	up to 14
Newborn	up to 7	up to 17
Up to 3 months	7–12	17–23
3–6 months	12–17	23–27
6–12 months	17–22	27–29
12–18 months	22–27	29–31
18–24 months	27–30	31–33
2 years	30–33	33–36
3 years	33–36	36–39
4 years	36–40	39–42
5 years	40–46	42–45

Old Navy

Size	Weight in Pounds	Length in Inches
0–3 months	7–12	19–23
3–6 months	12–17	23–27
6–12 months	17–22	27–29
12–18 months	22–27	29–31
18–24 months	27–30	31–33
2T/2–3 years	30–33	33–36
3T/2.25–4 years	33–36	36–39
4T/3.5–5 years	36–40	39–42
5T/4.5–5 years	40–46	42–45

Children's Place

Size	Weight in Pounds	Length in Inches
Preemie	up to 7	up to 18
0–3 months	7–11	18–22
3–6 months	11–15	22–25
6–9 months	15–18	25–27
12 months	18–22	27–29
18 months	22–26	29–31
24 months	26–29	31–34
36 months/3T	29–32	34–37
4T	32–35	37–40

Gymboree

Size	Weight in Pounds	Length in Inches
Up to 7 lbs	up to 7	up to 19
0–3 months	7–12	up to 23
3–6 months	12–17	23–25
6–12 months	17–23	25–29
12–18 months	22–27	29–31
18–24 months	27–30	31–33
2T	30–32	33–36
3/3T	32–35	36–39
4/4T	35–41	39–42
5/5T	41–46	42–45

Take a Closer Look

Be on the lookout for sizing guidelines at your favorite shops. Although most clothing will fall somewhere in the ranges listed above, get the most for your money by paying careful attention to sizing and by always buying clothes a little too big.

Consignment Shopping?

Bring these sizing charts along with you when you shop consignment or yard sales for easy reference.

103 ▌▌S▌ A Week's Worth of Quick and Easy Family-Friendly Meals

Making dinner for the family can be a challenge, but these time-saving taste bud pleasers will satisfy even the pickiest eaters, with minimal time and effort on your part. The best part: these recipes are flexible. If you're missing an ingredient (or two) the meal won't be compromised. There's also no tedious measuring. Unless otherwise noted, just throw in what you've got!

Sunday

Simple Slow Cooker Stew
Ingredients
   3 pounds beef stew meat, cut into cubes
   baby carrots, halved
   celery hearts, chopped
   baby new potatoes, quartered
   baby mushrooms
   2 onions, peeled and quartered
   28-ounce can of diced tomatoes
   1½ cups of water
   freeze-dried garlic, equivalent to one clove
   1 bay leaf
   1 teaspoon salt
   1 teaspoon black pepper
   1½ teaspoons paprika
   1½ teaspoons Worcestershire sauce

Directions
Combine all ingredients in a Crock-Pot. Cover and cook on low for 10 to 12 hours. Stir occasionally.

Monday

Make-Your-Own Pizza

Ingredients
    refrigerated pizza dough or sliced English muffins
    assorted pizza sauces
    assorted toppings
    shredded mozzarella cheese

Directions
Divide dough into individual portions and allow family members to roll out their own dough. Or give everyone an English muffin.

Let each person spread sauce on his or her dough or muffin and add toppings and cheese.

Bake as directed on dough packaging or toast muffins in a toaster oven until golden brown.

Tuesday

Terrific Baked Ziti

Ingredients
    1 box of ziti with lines
    1 large jar of pasta sauce
    1 24-ounce container of cottage cheese
    3 ounces of grated Parmesan cheese
    2 eggs
    1 pound shredded mozzarella cheese

To save time, use two disposable 8 x 8 or 9 x 9 pans—no dishwashing!

Directions

Boil pasta as directed on package. Line bottom of disposable pan with sauce. Combine cottage cheese, Parmesan cheese, and eggs in a large bowl. Mix well. Add sauce to mixture until it turns pink. Combine mixture with boiled pasta. Pour into pan. Top with remaining sauce. Top with shredded cheese. Cover with aluminum foil sprayed with cooking spray.

Bake covered at 350 degrees for 35 to 40 minutes. Remove foil the last ten minutes of baking. This recipe freezes and reheats really well.

Wednesday

Wacky and Warm Calzones

Ingredients

refrigerated pizza dough

fillings: leftovers, deli meat, sauce, cheese, vegetables, meat, dressings, anything!

Directions

Roll out refrigerated pizza dough on a floured surface. Cut dough into large, square pieces. Let family members choose their fillings. Fold up the ends of the dough to wrap in fillings.

Place calzones in baking pan or on a baking sheet.

Bake at 400 degrees for about 15 to 20 minutes or until golden brown.

Serve with a side salad.

Thursday

Tasty Tenders

Ingredients
  olive oil
  chicken tenders
  flour
  2 eggs, beaten
  bread crumbs
  marinara sauce or buffalo sauce
  Grated Parmesan cheese

Directions
Heat olive oil in a frying pan on medium-high heat. Dip chicken tenders first in flour, next in beaten eggs, and then in bread crumbs. Fry on each side for 2 minutes.

Place chicken in a baking pan. Top with marinara sauce and cheese for Parmesan tenders or with buffalo sauce for buffalo chicken tenders.

Bake at 350 degrees for 5 minutes or until juices run clear. Serve with fresh vegetables, dressing for dipping, and applesauce.

Friday

Fabulous Fajitas

Ingredients
  olive oil
  chicken tenders
  fajita seasoning
  onions, sliced
  green peppers, sliced
  tortilla wraps
  tomatoes, diced

lettuce, shredded

cheese, shredded

Directions

Heat olive oil in a frying pan on medium-high heat. Season tenders with fajita seasoning (Magic Seasonings Blends Fajita Magic is great!) and place in skillet. Add sliced onions and peppers. Cook chicken until juices run clear and the veggies are tender. Serve family style with tortillas.

Serve with tomatoes, lettuce, cheese, salsa, sour cream, tortilla chips, refried beans, and rice for a Mexican fiesta!

Saturday

Sensational Stir Fry

Ingredients

olive oil

chicken or beef, cut into thin strips

assorted vegetables, cut into bite-size pieces

sauce, such as sweet and sour, BBQ, soy, or teriyaki

Directions

Heat a pan or wok. Add a few tablespoons of olive oil. Add strips of meat and stir constantly until cooked through, about 5 minutes. Add vegetables. Add selected sauce. Cook until mixture is heated through. Serve with rice.

What Makes a Family Meal Family-Friendly?

Meals that allow you to alter the ingredients with minimal effort are great for families with differentiated taste buds. When children are allowed to choose their own toppings or ingredients, it can make their meal more attractive to them and eliminate mealtime struggles.

104 Three Tasty Treats That Every Mom Should Know How to Make

With more and more play groups and preschools requesting that moms take turns bringing snacks, having a few recipes for special treats up your sleeve can surely come in handy. While these three treats definitely don't rate high in nutritional value, they're completely off the charts in kid appeal and fun and are perfect for when you need to serve up a special-occasion treat.

Fruit Pizzas

Ingredients
- 1 package refrigerated sugar cookie dough
- 8-ounce package of softened cream cheese
- ½ cup sugar
- 2 teaspoons vanilla extract
- assorted seasonal sliced fruit

Directions
Bake cookies according to package directions. Combine cream cheese, sugar, and vanilla in a bowl. Mix well. Spread cream cheese "frosting" on individual cookies. Top with sliced fruit before serving. Kids can help spread cream cheese frosting and add sliced fruit for a make-your-own special treat.

Rice Cereal Treats

Ingredients
- 3 tablespoons butter

4 cups mini marshmallows

6 cups crisp rice cereal

Directions

Melt butter in a pan on low. Add marshmallows. Stir often and heat until melted together. Remove from heat and pour over rice cereal. Mix well. Spread mixture into a greased pan using wax paper. For fancier treats, you can mix dried fruits, colored candies, or food coloring in with the dry cereal prior to adding the melted marshmallows.

Cool the treats before cutting into squares.

You can also cut these treats with seasonal cookie cutters to fit any occasion.

Cups of Dirt

Ingredients

2 cups cold milk

1 package instant chocolate pudding

8-ounce package Cool Whip

1 package Oreo cookies, crushed

1 package gummy worms

Directions

Prepare pudding as directed. Mix in Cool Whip and half of the crushed Oreos. Line the bottom of small plastic drinking cups with crushed Oreos, saving some for the topping. Pour in pudding mixture. Top with remaining crushed Oreos. Refrigerate for at least one hour. Stick two gummy worms in each before serving.

Looking for Healthier Options?

Try these healthier favorites:

Ants on a Log: Fill celery with peanut butter and top with raisins.

Pinwheels: Spread peanut butter and jelly on a tortilla wrap, roll up, and slice into pinwheels.

Trail mix: Fill small plastic cups with O cereal, dried fruits, chocolate chips, and mini pretzels.

LIST 105 Ten Things a Mom Should Never Leave the House Without

In addition to your keys, wallet, cell phone, and sense of humor, there are some other essentials that you should never leave home without.

1. cash
2. bottle of water
3. nutrition bar
4. hand sanitizer
5. baby wipes
6. comb or brush
7. dental floss
8. pain reliever
9. pen
10. your calendar

Dental Floss?

In addition to being used to get gunk out of your teeth, dental floss can be used as string, thread, a makeshift hair band, or to clean out small crevices.

LIST 106 Twelve Sanity-Saving Stress Busters for Moms on the Go

A stressed-out mom can lead to an ineffective mom. These twelve stress busters are easy and affordable, and they can be effective in restoring you to your stress-free self.

1. Take a brisk walk.
2. Listen to inspirational music.
3. Pray.
4. Sip herbal tea.
5. Indulge in dark chocolate.
6. Vent to a good friend.
7. Sniff a soothing scent like lavender or eucalyptus.
8. Take a bubble bath after the kids go to bed.
9. Nap when the kids do.
10. Write in your journal.
11. Take a ten-minute time-out.
12. Share a good laugh with a friend who has a knack for making you chuckle.

Need More than a Moment?

Plan one Saturday a month when you and your spouse can split parenting duties for the day. Each of you takes half of the day to care for yourself. Get your hair cut, meet with a friend, go to the library, lose yourself in a book, or do whatever you find most refreshing.

LIST
107 Twenty Lists *You* Should Keep

Managing motherhood is a whole lot easier for moms who are organized. For busy, disorganized moms, keeping up-to-date lists can be the first step in the organization process. Lists help you plan, prioritize, and stop procrastinating. Above all, by using lists to stay organized, you can help keep your stress in check.

1. weekly to-do list
2. running grocery list
3. birthdays of families and friends
4. favorite Scripture verses
5. emergency contacts
6. school or child care information
7. your wish list
8. house rules
9. personal goals
10. questions to ask the doctor
11. items to buy
12. things that need fixing
13. school events and holidays
14. upcoming deadlines
15. appointments
16. frequently called phone numbers
17. addresses
18. holiday shopping
19. a master packing list for vacations
20. birthday wish lists for the kids

Wondering Where to Write Your Lists?

A spiral-bound notebook is a great place to keep your lists. Designate a page for each list. As you complete items on to-do lists, check them off, and when the list is completed, tear out the page.

Streamlining Motherhood Mania

Using a PDA or Pocket PC can provide one easy, amendable place to keep all your lists. Store phone numbers and addresses in your contact list and mark important dates, appointments, and deadlines in your electronic calendar.

108 Ten Instant, Mom-Tested, Mom-Approved Pick-Me-Ups

It's no secret that at times motherhood can be overwhelming. For instant rejuvenation, try these ten pick-me-ups.

1. Dance like nobody is watching.
2. Buy yourself a bouquet of flowers.
3. Do your hair.
4. Give yourself a facial.
5. Massage your scalp using circular motions.
6. Drink a glass of cool water.
7. Meditate on the Word.
8. Give yourself a manicure or a pedicure.
9. Wrap a warm heating pad around your neck.
10. Moisturize with a soothing scent.

Recipes for Relaxation

Oatmeal Mask: Make a paste from oatmeal and water. Apply to face and allow to dry. Remove with a damp cloth.

Exfoliating Mask: Mix 1 tablespoon of kosher salt with 3 tablespoons of olive oil. Gently rub into dry skin, avoiding eye area.

Egg White Mask: Separate an egg. Dip your clean hands into the egg white and smooth over face. Allow to dry. Let sit for fifteen minutes and rinse off.

109 Ten Tips for Balancing Home, Work, and Family

Managing kids, career, and home can be a hard act to juggle. In fact, I've written a whole book dedicated to the topic, called *Working Mom's 411*.[6] As a work-at-home mom myself, I've experienced this challenge. Here are my top tips for surviving.

1. *Solidify your child care arrangements.* Whether it's switching off child care responsibilities with your spouse, hiring a nanny, or sending your child to day care, having a solid, well thought-out child care plan can minimize stress and maximize work time.
2. *Prioritize your plans.* Get a good handle on what needs to be done and when. Prioritizing family needs, tasks, and work-related activities will help you be a more efficient mother, wife, and worker.
3. *Get organized.* Finding what you need when you need it is half the battle of accomplishing a task. I can't

stress this enough. Have a place for everything and put everything in its place.

4. *Have a routine.* Having a system for how things get done can help to keep your home running smoothly. Make a habit of shopping the same day each week and doing laundry on a schedule.

5. *Have a date night.* Take an evening for a time-out with your spouse. At least once a month, do something together, alone (see List 110).

6. *Insist on family meals.* The family meal is about more than eating. Dining together at the end of the day provides an opportunity for everyone to reconnect.

7. *Take time for you.* Even if it's a short escape to the bathroom to soak in a tub while reading a book, it's vital that you take a few moments each day to care for yourself and rejuvenate.

8. *Plan your meals in advance.* Sit down once each week to plan out your meals and make your weekly shopping list. You'll save time, money, and energy streamlining the meal-planning process.

9. *Delegate.* When people offer to help you out, take them up on the offer and don't be afraid to ask family and friends for help when you need it.

10. *Put God first.* No problem, no task, and no amount of chaos are too much for God. Invest in your relationship with him. The strength you'll find in him is priceless.

But seek first his kingdom and his righteousness, and all these things will be given to you as well.

Matthew 6:33

LIST 110 Ten Terrific and Affordable Time-Outs for Couples

Keeping the flame of your marriage burning is certainly easier if you make getting out together a regular priority. Take time away from the kids and enjoy an evening out together. Try these low-cost date ideas:

1. Spend the evening at a local bookstore.
2. Take a stroll in a park.
3. Enjoy time talking at a coffee house.
4. Take in a community theater, high school play, or college production.
5. Stay in and cook a fancy meal together.
6. Visit a museum.
7. Snuggle up and watch a movie, rented from the library or borrowed from a friend.
8. Enroll in dance lessons or other classes offered in your community.
9. Go roller-skating or ice-skating.
10. Visit an art gallery.

Best Day Dates

hiking
browsing a flea market or craft fair
going to a movie matinee

What about Child Care?

- Consider getting a few couples with kids together to do a monthly child care swap. Rotate taking care of each other's children so that every couple gets a turn to go out.

- Take family members up on their offer to babysit. Consider having the kids spend some quality time with their grandparents or other family members.
- Go out on a group date with another couple and split the cost of a sitter.

111 The Virtuous Wife

Do you ever find yourself wondering what makes a great wife? We can be thankful that God has provided a detailed answer to this question, and it can be found in the book of Proverbs. As you read this passage, apply it to your own life and seek to be the wife God describes.

The Virtuous Wife

A wife of noble character who can find?
　　She is worth far more than rubies.
Her husband has full confidence in her
　　and lacks nothing of value.
She brings him good, not harm,
　　all the days of her life.
She selects wool and flax
　　and works with eager hands.
She is like the merchant ships,
　　bringing her food from afar.
She gets up while it is still dark;
　　she provides food for her family
　　and portions for her servant girls.

She considers a field and buys it;
>   out of her earnings she plants a vineyard.
She sets about her work vigorously;
>   her arms are strong for her tasks.
She sees that her trading is profitable,
>   and her lamp does not go out at night.
In her hand she holds the distaff
>   and grasps the spindle with her fingers.
She opens her arms to the poor
>   and extends her hands to the needy.
When it snows, she has no fear for her household;
>   for all of them are clothed in scarlet.
She makes coverings for her bed;
>   she is clothed in fine linen and purple.
Her husband is respected at the city gate,
>   where he takes his seat among the elders of the
>   land.
She makes linen garments and sells them,
>   and supplies the merchants with sashes.
She is clothed with strength and dignity;
>   she can laugh at the days to come.
She speaks with wisdom,
>   and faithful instruction is on her tongue.
She watches over the affairs of her household
>   and does not eat the bread of idleness.
Her children arise and call her blessed;
>   her husband also, and he praises her:
"Many women do noble things,
>   but you surpass them all."
Charm is deceptive, and beauty is fleeting;
>   but a woman who fears the LORD is to be praised.
Give her the reward she has earned,
>   and let her works bring her praise at the city gate.

Proverbs 31:10–31

The Virtuous Wife of Today

So how does this Scripture translate for today's mom?

She seeks to be of good character and knows that a wife of good character is highly valued.

Her husband trusts her with his children, his home, and his finances. He trusts her to make wise family decisions. She fulfills all of his needs.

She consistently honors her husband, helps him to succeed, and wants only what is best for him.

She works cheerfully and diligently and ensures that the needs of the family and home are met. She chooses the best to bring into her home.

She grocery shops to find the best items at the best price.

She wakes early to get a jump start on her day. She prepares meals for her family.

She carefully considers her purchases and doesn't buy on impulse.

She is not lazy and takes care of her body, working to keep it fit.

She takes pride in her work, knows it is valuable, and does not quit until the work is completed.

She uses her hands constructively and gives her all to her work.

She helps others in need.

She dresses her children appropriately and is prepared to provide for their seasonal needs.

She doesn't put value in her appearance, but because of her hard work she has nice things and wears them well.

She is committed to her husband's success and knows the role he plays in his work.

She has enough for her family and makes a profit on her labor. She finds a way to help her family earn a profit, through making it easy for her husband to work or by earning a salary herself.

She is optimistic about her future and looks to the Lord for her strength and honor.

She is wise and kind. She thinks before she speaks. She has control of her tongue.

She pursues actively the best for her family and puts her family first.

She is a blessing to her family. Those who know her well praise her most.

Her strength of character is remarkable. Her husband sees her as above all others.

She fears the Lord consistently and honestly. She is in relationship with God.

Her work makes a difference. She is known for what she does, and the community praises and acknowledges her contributions.

LIST
112 Who's in Your Momtourage?

It used to take a village to raise a child. Today it takes a momtourage. All moms need a support network to raise their children successfully. Whether it is a friend to lean on, a child care provider you can totally trust, or a UPS delivery guy who always waits patiently until you get to the door, every mom needs someone sometime.

People to Recruit for Your Momtourage

your spouse
your extended family
your friends
your neighbors

your child care provider
your child's teacher
mothers with kids the same age
your child's pediatrician

Organizations to Include in Your Momtourage

your local church
your local mothers group
your local play group
your local nursing mothers support group
your local mothers of preschoolers group
your local mothers of twins club
your child's school or day care

Businesses to Include in Your Momtourage

your favorite restaurant that delivers
your local farm stand
UPS or any other package pickup and drop-off service
local grocery store delivery service
local pharmacy delivery service
your local twenty-four-hour pharmacy
Shutterfly or other Internet photo-ordering website
Vistaprint for ordering inexpensive (and often free!) invitations, announcements, and other printed items
Wholesale clubs like BJ's and Costco

You Know You're in a Momtourage When

Half of the kids you're driving to school aren't yours.

329

You prepare a meal for a new mom.

Your girlfriend calls and asks you to pick up something for her at the store while you're there.

A friend shows up with homemade cookies when she knows that you're down.

You can ask your neighbor friend to watch your kids when you're in a pinch.

What's a Momtourage?

A momtourage is the people, organizations, and businesses that help you get things done. It's your support system. It's made up of the people and places you know you can count on.

Notes

Preparing for Baby

1. Be sure to read the label of all over the counter medications carefully. Preparations other than original Tylenol may contain other ingredients in addition to acetaminophen that may not be safe for use during pregnancy.

2. http://www.americanpregnancy.org/pregnancyhealth/artificialsweetner.htm.

3. http://www.americanpregnancy.org/pregnancyhealth/artificialsweetner.htm.

4. The safety of Stevia is unknown when used as a sweetener during pregnancy and therefore should be avoided. http://www.americanpregnancy.org/pregnancyhealth/artificialsweetner.htm.

5. http://www.americanpregnancy.org/pregnancyhealth/artificialsweetner.htm.

6. http://www.transitiontoparenthood.com/ttp/parented/pregnancy/duedate.htm.

7. http://www.babiesonline.com/articles/pregnancy/a10monthpregnancy.asp.

8. http://www.dol.gov/esa/whd/fmla/.

9. http://www.americanbaby.com/ab/story.jhtml?storyid=/templatedata/ab/story/data/AB0804MaternityLeaveLaws.xml&categoryid=/templatedata/ab/category/data/YourLife_WorkAndMaternityLeave.xml&page=1.

10. http://info.insure.com/disability/shorttermdisability.html.

11. http://www.painfreebirthing.com/english/methods1.htm.

12. http://www.painfreebirthing.com/english/anatomy2.htm.

13. http://www.kellymom.com/nutrition/solids/delay-solids.html.

14. Petunia Pickle Bottom has an amazing diaper bag called the Boxy Backpack that has a detachable, washable changing pad. It has a water resistant liner that is great for spills, and the outer fabric is coated with a PVC free, water repellent

material that can be wiped down for easy cleaning. It also has tons of pockets and a dirty diaper pouch. www.petuniapicklebottom.com.

15. Baby Bjorn has a great seat called the Babysitter. It naturally translates your baby's movements into a gentle rocking motion. www.babybjorn.com.

16. http://www.cyh.com/HealthTopics/HealthTopicDetailsKids.aspx?p=335& np=152&id=1474#3.

17. http://www.drgreene.com/21_766.html.

18. Copyright Bob Hostetler. Used with the permission of the author. www .bobhostetler.com.

The First Year

1. Table compiled from information found in "Similac—A Guide to Feeding Your Baby" (Abbott Laboratories, 2008), 9.

2. http://www.llli.org/FAQ/milkstorage.html.

3. Table compiled from information found in "Similac—A Guide to Feeding Your Baby," 20.

4. http://www.4woman.gov/pub/BF.General.pdf.

5. Ibid.

6. http://www.llli.org/FAQ/enough.html.

7. Ibid.

8. Ibid.

9. http://www.pregnancy.org/article.php?sid=1453.

10. http://www.cdc.gov/breastfeeding/recommendations/vitamin_D.htm.

11. http://aappolicy.aappublications.org/cgi/content/full/pediatrics; 122/5/ 1142.

12. http://www.medscape.com/viewarticle/541952.

13. http://www.askdrsears.com/html/3/T032000.asp.

14. http://www.medscape.com/viewarticle/541952.

15. http://www.aap.org/publiced/BR_Solids.htm.

16. http://freshbaby.com.

17. http://www.wholesomebabyfood.com/tipYogurt.htm.

18. http://www.wholesomebabyfood.com/forbiddenbabyfood.htm.

19. "Weight Gain (Growth Patterns)," http://www.askdrsears.com/html/2/ t023600.asp.

20. Ibid.

21. "Average Weight Gain for Breastfed Babies," http://www.kellymom.com/ babyconcerns/growth/weight-gain.html.

22. Ibid.

23. http://www.cdc.gov/nchs/about/major/nhanes/growthcharts/Growthchart FAQs.htm.

24. http://www.childrenshospital.org/az/Site989/mainpageS989P0.html.

25. Check out the Grobag Baby Sleeping Bag (www.grobag.com). For baby wraps, check out the Miracle Blanket (www.miracleblanket.com) or the Kiddo-potamus SwaddleMe (www.kiddopotamus.com).

26. http://aappolicy.aappublications.org/cgi/reprint/pediatrics;116/5/1245 .pdf.

27. http://archpedi.ama-assn.org/cgi/content/abstract/162/10/963?lookupType
=volpage&vol=162&fp=963&view=shortArchPediatrAdolesc Med. 2008;162(10)
:963-968.

28. http://www.marchofdimes.com/pnhec/298_9542.asp.

29. The complete sleep training method is described by Richard Ferber, MD, in
his book *Solve Your Child's Sleep Problems* (New York: Fireside Book, 2006).

30. http://www.rhymes.org.uk/nursery-rhyme.htm.

The Toddler Years

1. http://www.fns.usda.gov/tn/Resources/Nibbles/fgp_nibbles.pdf.

2. http://www.childrenshospital.org/views/june06/sleep.html.

3. Based on calculations taken from http://www.keepkidshealthy.com/welcome/
conditions/failure_to_thrive.html.

4. http://rileychildrenshospital.com/parents-and-patients/caring-for-kids/
thetoddleryearschpt2.jsp.

5. Ibid.

The Preschool Years

1. http://kidshealth.org/parent/nutrition_fit/nutrition/preschool_snacks
.html.

2. http://www.mypyramid.gov/pyramid/printpages.html.

3. http://www.nytimes.com/2007/10/16/health/16well.html.

4. Calculations based on information found at http://www.keepkidshealthy
.com/welcome/conditions/failure_to_thrive.html.

5. http://nutrition.preschoolrock.com/index.php/understanding_nutrition/pre
schooler_calorie_needs_-_how_many_calories_does_your_preschooler_need.

6. http://www.movieguide.org/top-ten-lists.

7. http://www.melissaanddoug.com/.

8. http://www.aap.org/publiced/BR_WaterSafety.htm.

9. http://kidshealth.org/parent/growth/learning/preschool_music.html.

10. http://www.naeyc.org/academy/criteria/teacher_child_ratios.html.

11. http://www.naeyc.org/about/.

Family and Friends

1. http://www.safeyouth.org/scripts/faq/bullying.asp.

2. July 2008 *Parents* magazine, http://www.parents.com/parents/printableStory
.jsp?storyid=/templatedata/parents/story/data/1212425983582.xml.

3. http://www.opm.gov/Operating_Status_Schedules/fedhol/2008.asp.

4. Adapted from http://www.learningshopcatalog.com/the_ten_command
ments_for_kids_chart-p-131805.html.

5. http://www.christiananswers.net/q-eden/tolerance.html.

6. Ibid.

General Health and Safety

1. http://allergies.about.com/od/skinallergies/a/atopicderm1.htm.
2. http://allergies.about.com/od/childhoodallergies/a/atopicmarch.htm.
3. http://allergies.about.com/od/foodallergies/tp/topfoodallergyc.htm.
4. http://parenting.ivillage.com/gs/gshealth/0,,7mlhs9xf-2,00.html.
5. http://www.askdrsears.com/html/8/T082900.asp.
6. http://www.askdrsears.com/html/8/T081800.asp.
7. http://www.askdrsears.com/html/8/T083400.asp.
8. http://www.askdrsears.com/html/8/T083500.asp.
9. http://www.askdrsears.com/html/8/T083600.asp.
10. http://www.askdrsears.com/html/8/T082600.asp.
11. http://www.askdrsears.com/html/8/T082900.asp.
12. http://www.askdrsears.com/html/8/T084700.asp.
13. http://www.askdrsears.com/html/8/T083200.asp.
14. http://www.askdrsears.com/html/8/T085700.asp.
15. http://www.askdrsears.com/html/8/T082900.asp.
16. http://www.cdc.gov/vaccines/pubs/parents-guide/downloads/2008-parents-guide.pdf.
17. http://www.keepkidshealthy.com/WELCOME/immunizations/vaccines_and_autism.html
18. http://www.immunizationinfo.org/vaccine_components_detail.cfv?id=32.
19. http://www.mayoclinic.com/health/first-aid-burns/FA00022.
20. http://www.mayoclinic.com/health/first-aid-choking/FA00025.
21. http://www.thechildrenshospital.org/wellness/at_home/skin/injury.aspx.
22. http://www.mayoclinic.com/health/first-aid-bruise/FA00039.
23. The instructions are reprinted from http://depts.washington.edu/learncpr/index.html and used with permission from Dr. Mickey Eisenberg.
24. http://www.aap.org/publiced/BR_Medicine_OTC.htm.
25. http://www.aap.org/patiented/acetaminchart.htm.
26. http://www.aap.org/patiented/ibuprofenchart.htm.
27. http://aapnews.aappublications.org/cgi/content/full/30/4/12-a.
28. http://seatcheck.org/tips_safety_tips.html.
29. http://www.childrenshospital.org/views/december05/sleep.html.
30. http://www.southeastmissourihospital.com/safekids/statistics.htm.
31. http://www.sidsfamilies.com/index.php?sec=sidsstats.
32. http://www.cincinnatichildrens.org/svc/alpha/d/dpic/statistics.htm.
33. http://kidshealth.org/parent/general/sleep/cosleeping.html.
34. http://www.usa.safekids.org/tier2_rl.cfm?folder_id=174.
35. http://pediatrics.aappublications.org/cgi/content/abstract/117/3/e452.
36. http://www.blankees.com/house/plants/poisonous.htm.
37. http://www.cpsc.gov/cpscpub/prerel/prhtml07/07256.html.
38. http://www.americanheart.org/presenter.jhtml?identifier=3025002.
39. Ibid.
40. http://www.babycenter.com/0_infant-first-aid-for-choking-and-cpr-an-illustrated-guide_9298.bc.

41. If the answer to these first two questions is no, it's best to focus your child care search on centers that do perform background checks on all employees and hold current state licensing (if required) and accreditation with the National Association for the Education of Young Children (NAEYC). Visit www.naeyc .org to learn about accreditation for child care centers and to find an NAEYC accredited program in your area.

Saving Your Time, Money, and Sanity

1. http://www.cnpp.usda.gov/Publications/CRC/crc2007.pdf.

2. D. Lindsey Berkson annd John R. Lee, *Hormone Deception: How Everyday Foods and Products Are Disrupting Your Hormones—and How to Protect Yourself and Your Family* (McGraw Hill Professional, 2001), 113.

3. http://www.wholesomebabyfood.com/cost.htm.

4. http://www.rd.com/advice-and-know-how/16-ways-to-save-100/article12622 .html.

5. http://www.cnpp.usda.gov/Publications/CRC/crc2007.pdf.

6. Michelle LaRowe, *Working Mom's 411: How to Manage Kids, Career and Home* (Ventura, CA: Regal, 2009).

Michelle LaRowe is the 2004 International Nanny Association Nanny of the Year and is also the author of the Nanny to the Rescue! series and *Working Mom's 411: How to Manage Kids, Career & Home*. Michelle holds a bachelor of science degree in chemistry and a certificate in pastoral studies, and has spent more than a decade as a professional nanny and parenting consultant. She is an active member of the nanny community and currently serves as the executive director of the International Nanny Association. Michelle is regularly called on by the media as a "nanny expert" and has appeared on television (*The 700 Club*, NECN, FOX), has been featured in print (*USA Today*, the *Boston Globe*, *Better Homes and Gardens*) and is a regular columnist for several magazines, including *Families Online Magazine* and *Today's Pentecostal Evangel*. She and her husband, Jeff, reside in a seaside village of Cape Cod with their daughter, Abigail.

To learn more about Michelle, and to sign up to receive parenting tips, visit www.michellelarowe.com.